DATA STRUCTURES IN PYTHON

Algorithms and Data Structures Explained

THOMPSON CARTER

TABLE OF CONTENTS

INTRODUCTION

In today's fast-paced, technology-driven world, the ability to understand and efficiently manipulate data is an invaluable skill. Whether you're building web applications, optimizing algorithms, or designing complex systems, the performance and scalability of your solutions are often dictated by your choice of **data structures**. But what exactly are data structures, and why are they so important?

At its core, a **data structure** is a way of organizing and storing data in a computer so that it can be accessed and modified efficiently. The right data structure can dramatically improve the efficiency of your program, making it run faster and use memory more effectively. The wrong data structure, on the other hand, can cause your program to lag, crash, or waste precious resources.

In **Data Structures in Python: Algorithms and Data Structures Explained**, we will explore the fundamental concepts of data structures and algorithms, diving into the specifics of their implementation in Python. This book is designed for anyone eager to understand the building blocks of modern software engineering, from novice programmers to experienced developers looking to refine their skills. You don't need to be a computer science major to benefit from this guide—our focus is on clear, practical explanations and real-world examples that anyone can follow.

Why This Book?

Python is one of the most popular programming languages today, known for its simplicity and versatility. It's widely used in fields ranging from web development and data science to artificial intelligence and automation. Yet, despite its easy syntax, Python is still capable of implementing powerful, sophisticated data structures and algorithms. This book will show you how.

As you learn about each data structure—whether it's a simple list, a stack, a binary search tree, or a more advanced structure like a heap or a trie—you will gain an understanding of the strengths and weaknesses of each one. You will also learn how to implement these data structures in Python, giving you the tools to solve real-world problems with efficiency.

We will not only cover the basic data structures, but also the algorithms associated with them. An algorithm is simply a step-by-step procedure for solving a problem. By understanding how different algorithms interact with different data structures, you will be able to optimize your programs and solve complex challenges. From searching and sorting to dynamic programming and graph algorithms, we will provide clear, step-by-step guides to implementing each technique in Python.

The Structure of the Book

This book is divided into seven parts, each focusing on a key aspect of data structures and algorithms. Here's a quick overview of what you'll find in each section:

Part 1: Introduction to Data Structures and Algorithms

In this first section, we will introduce you to the concepts of data structures and algorithms. We'll explore their importance in programming and understand the core terminology, such as **Big-O notation**, which measures algorithm efficiency. By understanding these fundamentals, you'll be able to evaluate the performance of different algorithms and make more informed decisions about how to design your programs.

Part 2: Linear Data Structures

We'll begin by examining the most straightforward types of data structures: **arrays**, **lists**, **stacks**, **queues**, and **linked lists**. These are the building blocks for more complex data structures and are used extensively in a wide range of applications, from managing tasks in a queue to implementing undo/redo functionality in apps.

Part 3: Non-Linear Data Structures

Here, we'll move on to **trees** and **graphs**, which are more complex data structures that represent relationships between elements. These structures are used in everything from database indexing (e.g., B-trees) to web crawlers (using graphs to represent links between pages). We'll also cover **binary search trees (BST)** and **AVL trees**, which help us maintain ordered data efficiently.

Part 4: Hashing and Hash Tables

In this section, we'll cover **hashing**—a powerful technique that allows us to quickly store and retrieve data. By implementing **hash tables**, we can achieve near-instantaneous lookups, a critical feature in everything from caching to database indexing.

Part 5: Searching and Sorting Algorithms

With the knowledge of data structures in hand, we'll dive into how to search and sort data effectively. We'll cover **linear search**, **binary search**, and various sorting algorithms such as **quick sort** and **merge sort**, each with its own strengths and weaknesses depending on the problem at hand.

Part 6: Advanced Topics

This section will introduce you to **dynamic programming** and more advanced algorithms like **graph traversal** and **pathfinding algorithms** (e.g., Dijkstra's). These techniques are essential for solving complex problems that would otherwise be computationally prohibitive.

Part 7: Best Practices and Applications

Finally, we'll explore best practices for implementing data structures efficiently and discuss how they are applied in the real world. From databases to social networks to search engines, data structures are used extensively to solve everyday problems. We'll showcase some case studies, helping you understand how to apply the knowledge gained in the book to real-life systems.

What You Will Learn

By the end of this book, you'll have a deep understanding of the following:

- **Core data structures**: Learn how to implement arrays, stacks, queues, linked lists, trees, and hash tables in Python.
- **Algorithm design and efficiency**: Master algorithmic techniques such as searching, sorting, and dynamic programming. Learn how to analyze and optimize algorithm performance using **Big-O notation**.
- **Problem-solving strategies**: Gain practical experience by solving real-world problems and implementing common algorithms.
- **Real-world applications**: Understand how data structures are used in applications such as web development, databases, search engines, and social networks.

Why Should You Care?

As a programmer, understanding data structures and algorithms is more than just a technical skill—it's the foundation of problem-solving. Whether you're designing a system to handle millions of users, working with massive datasets, or optimizing a simple app, the way you structure your data will determine how effectively you can solve the problem at hand.

Mastering these concepts will not only improve your coding ability but also deepen your understanding of how modern software systems work. As you gain more experience with data structures and algorithms, you'll be able to recognize patterns, optimize solutions, and write cleaner, faster, and more efficient code.

Who Should Read This Book?

This book is intended for anyone looking to improve their understanding of data structures and algorithms. Whether you're a beginner eager to learn Python or an experienced developer looking to refine your skills, this book provides the knowledge and tools you need to succeed. Some of the audiences that will benefit from this book include:

- **Beginner programmers** who want to build a strong foundation in data structures and algorithms using Python.
- **Intermediate developers** who want to deepen their understanding of algorithmic thinking and optimize their existing code.
- **Students** preparing for technical interviews or exams that require a solid understanding of data structures and algorithms.
- **Professionals** working in fields like software engineering, data science, or machine learning who need to understand how to choose and implement efficient data structures.

In the world of software development, knowledge is power. By understanding the intricacies of data structures and algorithms, you're equipping yourself with the tools to solve some of the most complex problems in programming. This book will help you not only learn how to implement data structures in Python but also gain a deeper understanding of how to think algorithmically and optimize your solutions for maximum efficiency.

Let's embark on this journey together—by the end, you'll be well on your way to mastering the powerful art of data structures and algorithms. Happy coding!

CHAPTER 1: INTRODUCTION TO DATA STRUCTURES AND ALGORITHMS

What are Data Structures and Algorithms?

At the core of computer science lies the concept of data structures and algorithms. These two fundamental concepts are the building blocks for efficient programming and problem-solving. Let's break them down:

- **Data Structures** refer to the way data is organized, stored, and managed in a computer so that it can be accessed and manipulated efficiently. Think of a data structure as a container or framework that allows you to store and retrieve data in a specific way.

  Common examples include:

  - **Arrays**: Used for storing ordered collections of data.
  - **Linked Lists**: A series of connected nodes for efficient insertion and deletion.
  - **Stacks and Queues**: For managing tasks in a particular order (LIFO, FIFO).
  - **Trees**: Hierarchical structures like file systems or organizational charts.

13

- o **Graphs**: For modeling networks like social media, transportation systems, or web links.
- **Algorithms** are step-by-step procedures or formulas for solving problems. Algorithms operate on data structures, providing ways to search, sort, and modify the data efficiently. They define the logic and the steps required to achieve a specific task or solve a problem.

For example:

- o **Searching algorithms** (e.g., Binary Search) allow us to quickly find data within large datasets.
- o **Sorting algorithms** (e.g., Merge Sort, Quick Sort) enable us to arrange data in a specific order.
- o **Graph algorithms** (e.g., Dijkstra's Algorithm) help find the shortest path between points in a graph.

The combination of appropriate data structures and algorithms is what makes applications fast, efficient, and scalable.

Importance of Understanding Data Structures for Efficient Programming

A deep understanding of data structures and algorithms is crucial for writing efficient code. Here's why:

- **Efficiency**: Choosing the right data structure can significantly reduce the amount of time or space your program uses. For example, searching for an element in an unsorted list takes linear time ($O(n)$), but with a hash table or binary search tree, you can reduce this to constant or logarithmic time, respectively.

- **Scalability**: As the size of your data grows, the ability to scale your program becomes essential. A poor choice of data structure may result in performance bottlenecks when handling larger datasets. For instance, algorithms with inefficient time complexities, such as $O(n^2)$ (quadratic time), become impractical for larger datasets.

- **Maintainability**: Understanding data structures can help you design your program in a more organized and maintainable way. Properly chosen data structures make your code more modular and easier to read and update.

- **Problem-solving**: Algorithms are the tools you use to solve computational problems, and data structures help organize and manipulate data to apply these algorithms. Having a strong understanding of both empowers you to tackle complex problems efficiently.

Real-World Examples of How Data Structures and Algorithms are Used

Understanding data structures and algorithms becomes much more interesting when you see how they are applied in real-world scenarios. Let's look at some examples:

1. **Search Engines**:
   - o **Data Structures**: Search engines like Google use sophisticated data structures such as inverted indexes and hash tables to quickly locate and retrieve relevant information.
   - o **Algorithms**: PageRank, a core algorithm used by Google, ranks web pages based on their importance by analyzing links between pages, essentially treating the web as a graph.

2. **Social Media Networks**:
   - o **Data Structures**: Social networks (e.g., Facebook, Twitter) use graphs to model user connections and interactions. These graphs allow them to find mutual friends, suggest content, and track interactions.
   - o **Algorithms**: Graph traversal algorithms, like Breadth-First Search (BFS) and Depth-First Search (DFS), are used to traverse user connections, suggest friends, and recommend content.

3. **Navigation Systems**:

- o **Data Structures**: Maps and routes are represented as graphs with locations as nodes and roads as edges.
- o **Algorithms**: Algorithms like Dijkstra's or A* are used to find the shortest path between two locations.

4. **E-commerce**:
- o **Data Structures**: Hash tables or databases are used to store product details, user information, and transaction history.
- o **Algorithms**: Sorting algorithms (e.g., QuickSort) help arrange products by price or relevance, and search algorithms help find products in catalogs.

5. **Games**:
- o **Data Structures**: Games often use trees and graphs for things like game state management, movement, and AI pathfinding.
- o **Algorithms**: Pathfinding algorithms like A* are used to navigate characters through the game world, and game logic is implemented using dynamic programming to optimize performance.

Python's Role in Implementing Data Structures

Python, with its simplicity and readability, is an ideal language for learning and implementing data structures and algorithms. Here's why Python is great for data structures:

- **Readability**: Python's syntax is straightforward, making it easier to understand data structures and algorithms without the need to focus on complex syntax.

- **Built-in Data Structures**: Python comes with built-in data structures such as lists, dictionaries, sets, and tuples, which can be directly used in algorithm implementations. These structures offer efficient access and manipulation operations.

- **Libraries and Tools**: Python has a rich set of libraries that allow you to work with more complex data structures and algorithms. For example, collections.deque for queues and heapq for heaps. Python also has libraries like networkx for graph theory and numpy for numerical computations.

- **Versatility**: Python allows you to experiment and implement data structures in various ways. You can implement your own version of a linked list or use Python's built-in list for dynamic arrays. This flexibility encourages both learning and real-world application of data structures.

How This Book Will Approach Teaching Data Structures in Python

This book takes a **hands-on, practical approach** to learning data structures and algorithms in Python. Each chapter will focus on understanding a specific data structure or algorithm through:

- **Conceptual Explanation**: Clear, jargon-free explanations of what each data structure or algorithm is, and how it works.

- **Python Code Examples**: Real-world Python code implementations of each data structure and algorithm. This will not only demonstrate the theory behind the concept but also show you how to write the code efficiently.

- **Practical Applications**: We will apply each data structure to solve real-world problems. For example, how a stack can be used in undo operations or how a binary search tree can optimize search operations in a database.

- **Time and Space Complexity Analysis**: For each algorithm, we will analyze its performance using Big-O notation. This will help you choose the right algorithm for the right scenario.

- **Exercises and Challenges**: Each chapter will end with a set of exercises and challenges to reinforce the concepts you've learned. These exercises will range from basic to more advanced problems, ensuring a deep understanding of how to implement and optimize data structures.

By the end of this book, you will not only have a solid grasp of data structures and algorithms but also the ability to implement them effectively in Python to solve complex problems in your programming projects.

This chapter provides an overview of the crucial role data structures and algorithms play in programming, especially in Python. As we move through the following chapters, we will break down each structure and algorithm in detail, offering you the tools to optimize your code, improve performance, and tackle challenges in real-world applications.

CHAPTER 2: SETTING UP PYTHON FOR DATA STRUCTURES

In this chapter, we will cover the essential steps to set up your Python environment and prepare for implementing data structures and algorithms. The chapter will also introduce the fundamental Python data types, which will be essential for understanding more complex data structures later on. Let's get started.

---

1. Installing Python and Setting Up the Development Environment

Before we dive into Python data structures and algorithms, we need to ensure that Python is installed and ready to use. Here's how to set up the development environment:

Step 1: Installing Python

1. **Download Python**: Go to the official Python website and download the latest stable version of Python. The Python

Software Foundation releases updates regularly, so ensure you're downloading the latest version.

2. **Install Python**:

   o **Windows**: During installation, make sure to check the box that says **"Add Python to PATH"**. This ensures that you can run Python from the command line.

   o **Mac/Linux**: Python usually comes pre-installed on most Mac and Linux systems. However, if it's not installed or if you need an updated version, you can use package managers like **Homebrew** (for Mac) or **apt** (for Ubuntu).

3. **Verify Installation**: Open the terminal or command prompt and type the following command:

bash

python --version

This will display the installed Python version. If it shows a valid version (e.g., Python 3.10.0), Python is installed correctly.

Step 2: Installing Package Manager (pip)

Python comes with **pip**, a package manager that allows you to install additional libraries or packages. To verify if **pip** is installed, run:

bash

pip --version

If pip is installed, it will display the version number. If it's not installed, you can download it from the official pip website.

Step 3: Installing Virtual Environments

Using virtual environments allows you to isolate your Python projects and manage dependencies effectively. To create and activate a virtual environment, follow these steps:

1. **Create Virtual Environment**:

   bash

   python -m venv myenv

2. **Activate Virtual Environment**:
   - On Windows:

     bash

     myenv\Scripts\activate

   - On Mac/Linux:

     bash

     source myenv/bin/activate

2. Introduction to Python IDEs and Editors

While you can write Python code using a basic text editor, an **IDE (Integrated Development Environment)** or **code editor** enhances productivity by offering features like syntax highlighting, code completion, and debugging support. Here are some popular IDEs and editors for Python:

1. Visual Studio Code (VS Code)

- **Lightweight and highly customizable**.
- Offers features like IntelliSense (autocomplete), Git integration, debugging, and extensions for Python development.
- To set up, simply install **VS Code** from the official website, and then install the **Python extension** from the marketplace.
- **Recommended extensions**:
    - Python (by Microsoft)
    - Pylance (for enhanced IntelliSense)

2. PyCharm

- A popular IDE specifically designed for Python development, offering a full set of tools for coding, debugging, and testing.

- **Community version** is free, while the **Professional version** comes with additional features like web development support.
- PyCharm offers features like code suggestions, automatic formatting, and project navigation, making it ideal for complex Python applications.

3. Sublime Text

- A fast, minimalist code editor with great features for Python development.
- Supports syntax highlighting, plugins, and a powerful search function.
- Good for those who prefer a lighter editor compared to fully-featured IDEs.

4. Jupyter Notebooks

- Ideal for data science and mathematical operations.
- Allows you to combine code, visualizations, and text in an interactive environment.
- Great for prototyping, experimenting with algorithms, and testing small code snippets.

---

3. Working with Basic Python Data Types

Now that we have set up our environment, let's look at Python's **basic data types**, which are the foundation of more complex data structures. Understanding these fundamental data types is crucial before diving into custom data structures like lists, trees, and graphs.

1. Lists:

- A **list** in Python is an ordered, mutable (changeable) collection of elements.
- **Syntax:**

python

```
my_list = [1, 2, 3, 4]
```

- You can access, modify, and append elements in a list.

python

```
my_list[0]   # Access the first element
my_list.append(5)  # Add a new element to the list
```

2. Tuples:

- A **tuple** is an ordered collection of elements that is **immutable**, meaning it cannot be changed after creation.
- **Syntax:**

python

my_tuple = (1, 2, 3)

- Tuples are often used for fixed collections of values.

3. Dictionaries:

- A **dictionary** is an unordered collection of key-value pairs. It is mutable and allows fast lookup of values based on a unique key.
- **Syntax**:

python

my_dict = {"name": "Alice", "age": 25}

- You can access values by key and modify them.

python

```
my_dict["name"]   # Access the value of the key "name"
my_dict["age"] = 26  # Modify the value of "age"
```

4. Sets:

- A **set** is an unordered collection of unique elements. Sets are useful for operations like union, intersection, and difference.
- **Syntax**:

python

my_set = {1, 2, 3}

- Sets automatically remove duplicate values and do not maintain any order.

---

4. Introduction to Python's Built-in Data Structures

Python offers several built-in data structures that allow for the efficient storage and manipulation of data. In addition to lists, tuples, and dictionaries, Python provides the following data structures:

1. Queue:

- A **queue** is a collection of elements that follows the **FIFO (First In, First Out)** principle.
- Python does not have a built-in queue data structure, but you can use the **deque** from the collections module to implement one.

python

```
from collections import deque
queue = deque([1, 2, 3])
queue.append(4)  # Add element to the end
queue.popleft()  # Remove element from the front
```

2. Stack:

- A **stack** follows the **LIFO (Last In, First Out)** principle.
- You can use lists to implement a stack in Python.

python

```
stack = [1, 2, 3]
stack.append(4)  # Push element onto the stack
stack.pop()  # Pop element from the stack
```

3. Linked List:

- While Python does not have a built-in linked list, you can implement one yourself using classes or use the collections.deque for double-ended linked list functionality.

In this chapter, we covered the basic steps required to set up your Python development environment and introduced some of Python's core data types, such as lists, tuples, dictionaries, and sets. These fundamental data types will form the building blocks for implementing and understanding more advanced data structures as you progress through the book.

In the next chapter, we'll start working with more advanced data structures and explore how to implement and use them in Python. You'll also see how these data structures are essential for creating efficient algorithms, which we'll cover later in the book.

CHAPTER 3: BIG-O NOTATION AND ALGORITHM EFFICIENCY

In this chapter, we'll explore **Big-O notation**—a mathematical concept used to describe the **time complexity** and **space complexity** of algorithms. Understanding these concepts is crucial for analyzing how efficiently an algorithm performs as the size of the input data grows. We'll discuss common complexities and show how to measure and compare algorithm efficiency using real-world examples.

---

1. Understanding Time and Space Complexity

Time complexity and **space complexity** are two key metrics used to evaluate the performance of an algorithm. Both measure the resources required by an algorithm to execute:

- **Time complexity** measures how the runtime of an algorithm increases with respect to the input size.
- **Space complexity** measures how the memory usage of an algorithm increases with respect to the input size.

Time Complexity

Time complexity quantifies how the execution time of an algorithm changes as the size of the input grows. It helps determine how efficient an algorithm is in terms of runtime. For example, if you have an algorithm that performs a task a fixed number of times for every element in the input, its time complexity will depend on how many elements you have.

Space Complexity

Space complexity refers to how much extra space (memory) an algorithm uses as the input size grows. An algorithm that stores intermediate results or requires extra data structures to process input data will have higher space complexity.

---

2. The Importance of Algorithm Efficiency

As software systems grow in size and complexity, efficiency becomes increasingly important. In a large-scale application where millions of users interact with the system, even a slight inefficiency in an algorithm can result in performance bottlenecks. These inefficiencies can lead to increased processing time, excessive memory usage, or even system crashes. Understanding algorithm efficiency is essential for:

- **Optimizing performance**: Ensuring the algorithm runs as fast as possible, especially when dealing with large datasets.
- **Reducing memory usage**: Avoiding unnecessary memory consumption, especially in systems with limited resources like mobile devices or embedded systems.
- **Scalability**: Ensuring that an algorithm can handle increased loads as the input size grows.

---

3. Common Big-O Notations

Big-O notation is used to express the worst-case or upper bound of an algorithm's time or space complexity. Here are some common notations you'll encounter frequently when analyzing algorithms:

O(1) – Constant Time Complexity

An algorithm with **O(1)** time complexity means that the execution time does not depend on the size of the input data. The algorithm performs a constant number of operations, regardless of how large the input is.

Example:

python

```
def get_first_element(lst):
    return lst[0]
```

Here, accessing the first element of a list takes the same time, regardless of the list size.

O(n) – Linear Time Complexity

An algorithm with **O(n)** time complexity means that the execution time grows linearly with the size of the input. As the input size increases, the time taken by the algorithm grows proportionally.

Example:

python

```
def find_max(lst):
    max_val = lst[0]
    for num in lst:
        if num > max_val:
            max_val = num
    return max_val
```

In this case, we iterate through the entire list, so the time complexity is proportional to the size of the list.

O(n^2) – Quadratic Time Complexity

An algorithm with **O(n^2)** time complexity means that the execution time grows quadratically with the size of the input. This happens when an algorithm has nested loops where the number of iterations increases with the input size.

Example:

python

```
def bubble_sort(arr):
    for i in range(len(arr)):
        for j in range(len(arr) - 1):
            if arr[j] > arr[j + 1]:
                arr[j], arr[j + 1] = arr[j + 1], arr[j]
```

Here, we have two nested loops, each iterating over the entire array, resulting in quadratic time complexity.

O(log n) – Logarithmic Time Complexity

An algorithm with **O(log n)** time complexity reduces the problem size in each step, usually by half. This is typical in divide-and-conquer algorithms, such as binary search.

Example:

python

```
def binary_search(arr, target):
    low, high = 0, len(arr) - 1
    while low <= high:
        mid = (low + high) // 2
        if arr[mid] == target:
            return mid
        elif arr[mid] < target:
            low = mid + 1
        else:
```

```
    high = mid - 1
  return -1
```

In binary search, the input size is halved with each comparison, making the algorithm run in logarithmic time.

O(n log n) – Linearithmic Time Complexity

An algorithm with **O(n log n)** time complexity often involves dividing the input into smaller parts and performing some operation on them. It's commonly seen in efficient sorting algorithms like quicksort and mergesort.

Example:

python

```
def merge_sort(arr):
  if len(arr) <= 1:
    return arr
  mid = len(arr) // 2
  left = merge_sort(arr[:mid])
  right = merge_sort(arr[mid:])
  return merge(left, right)
```

The divide-and-conquer approach in merge sort gives it a time complexity of **O(n log n)**.

O(2^n) – Exponential Time Complexity

An algorithm with **O(2^n)** time complexity doubles the work with each additional element in the input. This is seen in algorithms that try all possible solutions, such as brute-force solutions to the traveling salesman problem.

Example:

python

```
def fibonacci(n):
    if n <= 1:
        return n
    return fibonacci(n - 1) + fibonacci(n - 2)
```

Here, the function calls itself twice for every number, leading to exponential growth in the number of function calls.

O(n!) – Factorial Time Complexity

An algorithm with **O(n!)** time complexity grows extremely fast, and is often encountered in problems that involve generating all possible permutations of a set (e.g., solving the traveling salesman problem with brute force).

---

4. Real-World Examples of Algorithm Performance

Understanding algorithm performance is not just theoretical. Let's look at a couple of real-world scenarios where time and space complexity directly impact performance:

1. **Web Searching**: In web search engines, algorithms must quickly sift through vast amounts of data. A simple linear

search (O(n)) would not work efficiently on billions of web pages. Instead, more sophisticated algorithms with logarithmic (O(log n)) or even linearithmic (O(n log n)) time complexity are used to index and retrieve results quickly.

2. **Social Media Feeds**: Social media platforms use algorithms to filter and display posts in real-time. These algorithms need to process vast amounts of data quickly. Efficient sorting (e.g., O(n log n)) and searching (e.g., O(log n)) algorithms are crucial for providing users with the most relevant content in their feeds without delay.

3. **E-commerce Search and Recommendation**: E-commerce websites use recommendation algorithms that sort products and recommend items based on user behavior. These algorithms use time-efficient sorting and searching techniques like merge sort (O(n log n)) to ensure that the user gets relevant recommendations quickly.

---

5. Measuring and Comparing Algorithm Efficiency

To measure the efficiency of an algorithm, we can compare the time complexity of different approaches to solving the same problem. For instance, consider sorting:

- **Bubble Sort (O(n^2))**: Simple but inefficient for large datasets because it repeatedly compares adjacent elements, resulting in quadratic time complexity.

- **Merge Sort (O(n log n))**: More efficient because it divides the data and sorts in parallel, yielding linearithmic time complexity, which is much faster for large datasets.

While Big-O notation gives us a high-level understanding of algorithm efficiency, **real-world performance** can vary based on implementation details, hardware, and input data characteristics. This is why **benchmarking**—timing the execution of algorithms on sample data—is a good way to compare how different algorithms perform in practice.

Example: Benchmarking Sorting Algorithms

python

```
import time

arr = [5, 2, 9, 1, 5, 6]
start_time = time.time()
bubble_sort(arr)
print("Bubble Sort Time: %s seconds" % (time.time() - start_time))


arr = [5, 2, 9, 1, 5, 6]
start_time = time.time()
merge_sort(arr)
print("Merge Sort Time: %s seconds" % (time.time() - start_time))
```

In this chapter, we introduced the concept of **Big-O notation** and its role in analyzing algorithm performance. Understanding time and space complexity is crucial for writing efficient algorithms, especially when dealing with large datasets or performance-sensitive applications. By learning to recognize and calculate the complexity of different algorithms, you'll be equipped to make informed decisions on which algorithm to use based on the specific requirements of your program.

In the next chapter, we'll start applying these concepts to common data structures and explore how to implement them in Python efficiently.

CHAPTER 4: ARRAYS AND LISTS

In this chapter, we'll delve into one of the most fundamental data structures used in programming: **arrays and lists**. These linear data structures are essential for organizing and manipulating collections of elements, and understanding their implementation and use cases is crucial for building efficient programs.

1. What is an Array, and How Do Arrays Differ from Lists?

Arrays and **lists** are both used to store multiple elements in a single variable, but they have distinct characteristics. Let's break down the two:

Array:

An **array** is a collection of elements, all of the same type, stored in contiguous memory locations. Arrays are fixed in size, meaning that the number of elements in an array must be determined when the array is created, and it cannot be resized later without creating a new array. Arrays are commonly used in languages like **C** and **Java**, where memory management is more manual.

Key Characteristics of Arrays:

- **Fixed Size**: Once an array is created, its size cannot be changed.
- **Homogeneous**: All elements in an array are of the same type (e.g., integers, strings, etc.).
- **Direct Access**: Elements in an array can be accessed directly using an index, making access time constant ($O(1)$).

List:

In **Python**, the closest equivalent to an array is a **list**. Unlike arrays, Python lists are **dynamic**, meaning they can grow or shrink in size as needed. They can hold elements of different data types (integers, strings, objects, etc.), making them more flexible than arrays.

Key Characteristics of Lists:

- **Dynamic Size**: Lists can grow and shrink as needed.
- **Heterogeneous**: Lists can hold elements of different types (e.g., integers, strings, or even other lists).
- **Direct Access**: Like arrays, lists allow direct access to elements via indices ($O(1)$).

Comparison of Arrays vs. Lists in Python:

While arrays in some languages are fixed in size and store homogeneous data, **Python lists** can store both homogeneous and heterogeneous data and are dynamic in nature. Python does not have a built-in array type like other languages, but the **array module** provides an array-like structure with fixed data types and more memory efficiency.

---

2. Implementing Arrays and Lists in Python

Python Lists:

Python provides a **built-in list** type, which is highly flexible and can grow or shrink in size. It allows you to store multiple items in a single variable.

Creating a List:

python

```python
# Creating a list with integers
my_list = [1, 2, 3, 4, 5]
```

```python
# Creating a list with mixed data types
mixed_list = [1, "Hello", 3.14, True]
```

Accessing Elements in a List: Lists are zero-indexed, meaning the first element is at index 0, the second at index 1, and so on.

python

```python
# Accessing the first element
print(my_list[0])  # Output: 1
```

```python
# Accessing the last element
print(my_list[-1])  # Output: 5
```

Adding Elements to a List: You can append new elements to a list using append(), or insert elements at a specific index using insert().

python

```python
# Appending an element to the end
my_list.append(6)
```

```python
# Inserting an element at index 2
my_list.insert(2, "new element")
```

Removing Elements from a List: You can remove elements using remove() (which removes the first occurrence of a value), pop()

(which removes an element at a specific index), or clear() (which removes all elements).

python

```
# Removing the first occurrence of a specific element
my_list.remove("new element")
```

```
# Removing and returning the last element
last_element = my_list.pop()
```

Python Arrays:

Python also provides an array module, which is more efficient for storing homogeneous data types. Unlike lists, arrays are typically used when you need to store large amounts of data and want more control over memory usage.

To work with arrays, you need to import the array module:

python

```
import array
```

```
# Creating an array of integers
arr = array.array('i', [1, 2, 3, 4, 5])
```
Here, the 'i' indicates that the array will store **integers**.

Basic Operations on Arrays:

python

```
# Adding an element to an array
arr.append(6)
```

```
# Inserting an element at index 2
arr.insert(2, 9)
```

```
# Removing an element from the array
arr.remove(4)
```

```
# Accessing an element
print(arr[2])  # Output: 9
```

Note: Python arrays are less commonly used than lists, and are generally more efficient when working with numeric data where memory management is critical.

---

3. *Common Operations: Insertion, Deletion, Traversal, and Searching*

Here, we'll cover some essential operations that are frequently performed on arrays and lists in Python:

Insertion:

Insertion adds a new element to the data structure. In lists, this can be done using append(), insert(), or list concatenation.

- **append()**: Adds an element to the end of the list (O(1)).
- **insert()**: Adds an element at a specific position in the list (O(n) in the worst case).

Deletion:

Deletion removes an element from the list or array.

- **remove()**: Removes the first occurrence of a specified element (O(n)).
- **pop()**: Removes the element at the specified index or the last element (O(1)).
- **clear()**: Removes all elements from the list (O(n)).

Traversal:

Traversal involves iterating over each element of the list or array to process them, often done using loops like for or while.

Example:

python

```
for item in my_list:
    print(item)
```

Searching:

To search for an element in a list or array, you can use the in operator (which checks if an element exists in the list) or a more specific search method like index().

Example:

python

```
# Checking if an element exists in the list
```

```
if 3 in my_list:
    print("Found 3!")
```

```
# Getting the index of an element
index_of_three = my_list.index(3)
```

---

4. Real-World Applications: Storing Collections of Similar Elements

Arrays and lists are foundational data structures used in many real-world applications. Let's look at a few examples:

1. Storing a List of Student Names:

A list of students' names in a classroom or course registration system can be stored using a Python list.

python

```
students = ["Alice", "Bob", "Charlie", "David"]
```

This allows quick access, modification, and management of the list of students.

2. Temperature Recordings:

If you're building a system to track temperature readings, an array or list can be used to store daily temperature data for efficient analysis and reporting.

python

```
temperatures = [22, 25, 19, 21, 23, 26]
```

This can then be used to calculate the average temperature, find trends, or plot graphs.

3. Game Data:

In a video game, you might store the positions of all active enemies or players in a list for easy updates during the game loop.

python

```
enemy_positions = [(x, y), (x2, y2), (x3, y3)]
```
This allows the game to easily track and update each enemy's location during gameplay.

Arrays and lists are some of the most fundamental data structures in Python, and mastering their usage is crucial for any programmer. Lists, in particular, are widely used because of their flexibility and ease of use in Python. By understanding how to implement these data structures and perform basic operations such as insertion, deletion, traversal, and searching, you'll be well on your way to solving a variety of programming problems efficiently.

In the next chapter, we will dive deeper into another important linear data structure: **Stacks and Queues**, exploring their applications and how to implement them in Python.

CHAPTER 5: STACKS

In this chapter, we'll explore one of the most fundamental and widely used data structures in computer science: **Stacks**. Stacks are often utilized for managing tasks that require a **Last In, First Out (LIFO)** order of operations, such as managing undo operations in applications, handling function calls in programming, and tracking browser history. By understanding how to implement and use stacks, you will be able to solve a variety of real-world problems efficiently.

1. Definition and Uses of a Stack

A **stack** is a linear data structure that follows the **Last In, First Out (LIFO)** principle. This means that the last element added to the stack is the first one to be removed. Think of a stack of plates: you add plates to the top, and when you remove a plate, you take the top plate first.

Key Characteristics of a Stack:

- **LIFO Order**: The last element added is the first one to be removed.
- **Operations**: A stack typically supports three primary operations:
    o **Push**: Add an element to the top of the stack.
    o **Pop**: Remove the top element from the stack.
    o **Peek**: View the top element without removing it.

Common Uses of Stacks:

Stacks are used in many different scenarios in both **real-world applications** and **algorithm design**. Here are a few examples:

- **Undo/Redo Operations**: When you perform an action, it is pushed onto a stack. To undo an action, you pop the most recent item.

- **Browser History**: The history of visited web pages is stored in a stack, allowing the user to navigate back and forward through pages in a LIFO order.
- **Function Calls (Call Stack)**: When a function is called in most programming languages, its state (such as local variables) is pushed onto a call stack. When the function completes, the state is popped from the stack.
- **Expression Evaluation**: Stacks are used in algorithms for evaluating expressions like infix, postfix, and prefix notations.

---

2. Implementing a Stack Using Lists in Python

In Python, stacks can be easily implemented using the built-in list data type. Python lists support operations that work perfectly with the LIFO principle, such as append() (to push) and pop() (to remove).

Basic Stack Operations in Python:

Let's implement a simple stack using Python's list and walk through the main stack operations.

python

```
# Initialize an empty stack
stack = []


# Push operation: Adding elements to the stack
```

```
stack.append(1)  # Stack: [1]
stack.append(2)  # Stack: [1, 2]
stack.append(3)  # Stack: [1, 2, 3]


# Pop operation: Removing the top element
top_element = stack.pop()  # Stack: [1, 2], top_element: 3


# Peek operation: Viewing the top element without removing it
top_element = stack[-1]  # Stack: [1, 2], top_element: 2
```

Explanation of Operations:

- **Push**: The append() method adds an element to the end of the list, which is treated as the "top" of the stack.

- **Pop**: The pop() method removes and returns the last element of the list, which is the "top" of the stack.

- **Peek**: We use stack[-1] to view the top element without removing it. This gives us the last element in the list, which corresponds to the top of the stack.

Empty Stack Handling:

Before performing a pop() or peek(), it's a good practice to check if the stack is empty to avoid errors. You can do this with a simple condition:

python

```
if stack:
    top_element = stack.pop()
```

```
else:
    print("Stack is empty")
```

---

3. Stack Operations: Push, Pop, Peek

Let's break down the stack operations in more detail, using real-world examples to solidify the concepts.

Push Operation:

The **push** operation adds an element to the top of the stack. This can be done using Python's append() method for lists.

Example: Pushing numbers onto the stack.

python

```
stack = []
stack.append(10)  # Stack: [10]
stack.append(20)  # Stack: [10, 20]
stack.append(30)  # Stack: [10, 20, 30]
```

Pop Operation:

The **pop** operation removes the top element from the stack and returns it. If the stack is empty, trying to pop an element will raise an error (unless handled).

Example: Popping the top element from the stack.

python

```
top = stack.pop()  # Removes 30, Stack: [10, 20]
```

```
print(top)  # Output: 30
```

Peek Operation:

The **peek** operation returns the top element without removing it. This is useful when you need to check the current state of the stack without modifying it.

Example: Peeking at the top element.

python

```
top = stack[-1]  # Returns 20 without removing it
print(top)  # Output: 20
```

---

4. Practical Examples: Undo/Redo, Browser History

Undo/Redo:

Imagine you're building a simple text editor that supports undo and redo. You can use a stack to store the previous states of the document. When the user performs an action (e.g., typing), you push the current state onto a stack. To undo an action, you pop the last state from the stack and revert to it.

python

```
# Stack for undo functionality
undo_stack = []
redo_stack = []
```

```
# Perform an action and push the current state onto the undo stack
current_state = "Hello"
undo_stack.append(current_state)


# Undo: Pop the last action from the undo stack and push it onto the redo stack
last_state = undo_stack.pop()
redo_stack.append(last_state)
```

Browser History:

When you visit a webpage, the current URL is pushed onto a stack. When you press the back button, the most recent URL is popped from the stack, allowing you to navigate backward in your history.

python

```
# Browser history stack
history_stack = []


# Visiting a new page
history_stack.append("https://www.example.com")


# Navigating backward: Popping the last visited URL
last_visited = history_stack.pop()
print(last_visited)  # Output: https://www.example.com
```

---

5. Real-World Applications of Stacks

1. Function Call Management:

In most programming languages, function calls are managed using a stack. When a function is called, its local variables and return address are pushed onto the stack. When the function completes, the stack is popped to return control to the calling function.

2. Expression Evaluation:

Stacks are commonly used to evaluate expressions, especially in postfix or prefix notation. In postfix notation, operators follow operands, so stacks are ideal for evaluating such expressions step by step.

Example (Postfix Evaluation):

python

```python
# Postfix expression: 3 4 + 2 * (equivalent to (3 + 4) * 2)
stack = []
expression = [3, 4, '+', 2, '*']

for token in expression:
    if isinstance(token, int):
        stack.append(token)
    elif token == '+':
        b = stack.pop()
        a = stack.pop()
        stack.append(a + b)
    elif token == '*':
        b = stack.pop()
        a = stack.pop()
        stack.append(a * b)
```

print(stack[-1]) # Output: 14

3. Balancing Parentheses:

A common algorithm that uses a stack is to check if parentheses (or other brackets) are balanced in an expression. For example, checking if "(a + b) * [c + (d - e)]" is balanced.

python

```
def is_balanced(expression):
    stack = []
    for char in expression:
        if char in '([{':
            stack.append(char)
        elif char in ')]}':
            if not stack:
                return False
            top = stack.pop()
            if char == ')' and top != '(':
                return False
            if char == ']' and top != '[':
                return False
            if char == '}' and top != '{':
                return False
    return len(stack) == 0


print(is_balanced("(a + b) * [c + (d - e)]"))  # Output: True
```

Stacks are a fundamental and powerful data structure used in many real-world applications. They provide an efficient way to manage and organize data with the **Last In, First Out** (LIFO) principle. From managing function calls in programming to handling undo/redo operations in applications, stacks are indispensable for many tasks.

In this chapter, we've covered the basics of stacks, including their definition, operations, and real-world applications. We've also implemented stacks in Python using lists, providing a hands-on understanding of how stacks work in practice.

In the next chapter, we will explore **Queues**, another important linear data structure that operates on the **First In, First Out (FIFO)** principle.

CHAPTER 6: QUEUES

In this chapter, we will explore **Queues**, a linear data structure that follows the **First In, First Out (FIFO)** principle. A queue is like a waiting line at a checkout counter or a line of tasks waiting to be processed by a computer system. The first item that enters the queue is the first one to leave. Queues are essential in many computing systems where tasks need to be processed in the order they arrive. You will learn about the basic operations of a queue, how to implement one in Python, and practical real-world use cases for queues.

---

1. Understanding the Concept of a Queue

A **queue** is a collection of elements that supports two main operations: **enqueue** and **dequeue**.

- **Enqueue**: This operation adds an element to the back (or rear) of the queue.
- **Dequeue**: This operation removes an element from the front of the queue.

Queues follow the **First In, First Out (FIFO)** order, meaning that the first element added to the queue will be the first one to be removed.

Key Characteristics of a Queue:

- **FIFO (First In, First Out)**: The order in which elements are processed is based on their arrival, i.e., the first element enqueued is the first one to be dequeued.
- **Operations**:
    - **Enqueue**: Adding an element to the end (rear) of the queue.

- o **Dequeue**: Removing an element from the front of the queue.

- o **Front**: Accessing the element at the front of the queue without removing it.

- o **Rear**: Accessing the element at the rear of the queue without removing it.

Real-World Applications of Queues:

Queues are used in a variety of real-world scenarios:

- **Scheduling Tasks**: In operating systems, tasks are scheduled in a queue for processing. The first task to arrive is the first one to be executed.

- **Job Queues**: In print servers, print jobs are handled in a queue. The first print job received is the first to be printed.

- **Request Handling**: Web servers often use queues to handle incoming client requests in the order they are received.

- **Customer Service**: A call center uses a queue to manage customer support requests, serving customers in the order their calls arrive.

---

2. Implementing a Queue in Python

In Python, we can implement a queue using the built-in collections.deque class, which is optimized for fast appends and pops from both ends of a collection. This makes it a perfect choice for implementing a queue, as the append() operation adds elements to the rear of the queue, and the popleft() operation removes elements from the front.

Queue Implementation Using collections.deque:

python

```python
from collections import deque

# Create an empty queue
queue = deque()

# Enqueue operation: Adding elements to the rear of the queue
queue.append(10)  # Queue: [10]
queue.append(20)  # Queue: [10, 20]
queue.append(30)  # Queue: [10, 20, 30]

# Dequeue operation: Removing the front element
front_element = queue.popleft()  # Queue: [20, 30], front_element: 10

# Front operation: Viewing the front element without removing it
front_element = queue[0]  # Queue: [20, 30], front_element: 20

# Rear operation: Viewing the rear element without removing it
rear_element = queue[-1]  # Queue: [20, 30], rear_element: 30

# Output current state of the queue
print(queue)  # Output: deque([20, 30])
```

- **Enqueue (append)**: Adds an element to the rear (end) of the queue.
- **Dequeue (popleft)**: Removes and returns the element from the front of the queue.
- **Front**: We access the element at the front using the index queue[0].
- **Rear**: We access the element at the rear using the index queue[-1].

Empty Queue Handling:

Just like in stacks, you should check whether the queue is empty before performing dequeue or front operations. This prevents errors.

python

```
if queue:
    front_element = queue.popleft()
else:
    print("Queue is empty")
```

3. Queue Operations: Enqueue, Dequeue, Front, Rear

Let's dive deeper into the operations that make up a queue.

Enqueue Operation:

The **enqueue** operation adds an element to the end of the queue.

python

```
queue = deque()
queue.append(5)  # Queue: [5]
queue.append(10)  # Queue: [5, 10]
queue.append(15)  # Queue: [5, 10, 15]
```

Dequeue Operation:

The **dequeue** operation removes the element from the front of the queue. It also returns the element removed.

python

```
front = queue.popleft()  # Queue: [10, 15], front: 5
print(front)  # Output: 5
```

Front Operation:

The **front** operation gives you access to the first element of the queue without removing it.

python

```
front = queue[0]  # Accessing the first element without removing it
print(front)  # Output: 10
```

Rear Operation:

The **rear** operation gives you access to the last element of the queue without removing it.

python

```
rear = queue[-1]  # Accessing the last element without removing it
print(rear)  # Output: 15
```

---

4. Real-World Examples of Queues

1. Task Scheduling in Operating Systems:

Operating systems often use queues to manage tasks that need to be processed. Each task or process is added to the queue in the order it is received. The system then processes tasks in the same order, ensuring fairness and efficiency.

python

```
# Simulating a task scheduler with a queue
task_queue = deque()

# Enqueue tasks
task_queue.append("Task 1")
task_queue.append("Task 2")
task_queue.append("Task 3")

# Process tasks in the order they were added
while task_queue:
    current_task = task_queue.popleft()
    print(f"Processing: {current_task}")
```

Output:

arduino

Processing: Task 1

Processing: Task 2

Processing: Task 3

2. Web Request Handling:

Web servers use queues to handle incoming requests. When a request is made, it is added to the queue. The server processes requests in the order they are received, ensuring fair and timely responses.

python

```python
# Simulating a web server request queue
request_queue = deque()

# Enqueue requests
request_queue.append("Request 1")
request_queue.append("Request 2")
request_queue.append("Request 3")

# Process requests in the order they were received
while request_queue:
    current_request = request_queue.popleft()
    print(f"Processing: {current_request}")
```

Output:

makefile

Processing: Request 1

Processing: Request 2

Processing: Request 3

3. Customer Service Call Center:

In a customer service call center, calls are queued in the order they arrive. The first customer to call is the first to be served.

python

```python
# Simulating a customer service queue
customer_queue = deque()

# Enqueue calls
customer_queue.append("Customer 1")
customer_queue.append("Customer 2")
customer_queue.append("Customer 3")

# Serve customers in the order they called
while customer_queue:
    current_customer = customer_queue.popleft()
    print(f"Serving: {current_customer}")
```

Output:

makefile

```
Serving: Customer 1
Serving: Customer 2
Serving: Customer 3
```

Queues are essential data structures that play a crucial role in many real-world applications, from task scheduling and web request handling to customer service operations. By understanding how queues work and how to implement them in Python using collections.deque, you are equipped with a powerful tool for efficiently managing tasks and data.

In this chapter, we've explored the key operations of a queue, implemented a simple queue in Python, and looked at practical examples of how queues are used in the real world. Understanding queues is fundamental to mastering algorithms and solving a wide range of problems in computer science and software development.

In the next chapter, we will move on to **Linked Lists**, another important data structure that allows for efficient insertion and deletion operations.

CHAPTER 7: LINKED LISTS

In this chapter, we will explore **Linked Lists**, a dynamic and flexible data structure that can be used to organize data in ways that are not possible with arrays. Unlike arrays, linked lists do not store elements in contiguous memory locations, making them more efficient in scenarios where frequent insertion and deletion of elements occur. Linked lists are foundational in understanding more advanced data structures and algorithms, as well as memory management.

---

1. What is a Linked List and How Is It Different from Arrays?

A **linked list** is a linear data structure in which each element (called a node) contains two parts:

- **Data**: The actual content or value of the node.
- **Next (or Pointer)**: A reference (or pointer) to the next node in the list.

In contrast to **arrays**, which store elements in contiguous memory locations, linked lists store elements in non-contiguous memory locations. Each node points to the next one, which makes insertion and deletion operations efficient, especially when the list is large or when data is frequently inserted or deleted at different positions.

Key Differences Between Arrays and Linked Lists:

- **Memory Allocation**:
    - o Arrays use contiguous memory locations.
    - o Linked lists use non-contiguous memory locations and dynamically allocate memory as needed.

- **Size:**
  - o Arrays have a fixed size, determined at creation.
  - o Linked lists are dynamic, meaning they can grow or shrink in size during runtime.
- **Access Time:**
  - o Arrays provide constant-time access to elements by index (O(1)).
  - o Linked lists require traversal from the head node to find an element (O(n)).
- **Insertion/Deletion:**
  - o Arrays require shifting elements for insertion or deletion (O(n)).
  - o Linked lists allow efficient insertion and deletion at any position (O(1)), as long as we have a reference to the node.

---

2. Implementing Singly Linked Lists in Python

A **singly linked list** is a type of linked list where each node points to the next node in the list, and the last node's next pointer is None.

Node Class:

Each node in the linked list will be an instance of the Node class, which holds two attributes: the data and the next pointer.

python

```python
class Node:
    def __init__(self, data):
        self.data = data  # Stores the node's data
        self.next = None  # Points to the next node (default is None)
```

Linked List Class:

The LinkedList class manages the list, providing methods for insertion, deletion, and traversal.

python

```python
class LinkedList:
    def __init__(self):
        self.head = None  # The head node is initially None (empty list)

    # Insertion at the end of the list
    def append(self, data):
        new_node = Node(data)
        if not self.head:
            self.head = new_node  # If the list is empty, make the new node the head
        else:
            current = self.head
            while current.next:
                current = current.next  # Traverse to the last node
            current.next = new_node  # Set the next of the last node to the new node

    # Traversal of the list
    def traverse(self):
        current = self.head
        while current:
```

```python
        print(current.data, end=" -> ")
        current = current.next
    print("None")


# Deletion of a node by value
def delete(self, data):
    current = self.head
    if current and current.data == data:
        self.head = current.next  # Move the head to the next node
        current = None
        return


    prev = None
    while current and current.data != data:
        prev = current
        current = current.next


    if current is None:  # The value is not found
        print("Node with value", data, "not found.")
        return


    prev.next = current.next  # Remove the node from the list
    current = None
```

Example Usage:

python

```python
# Create a linked list
ll = LinkedList()


# Append nodes
```

```
ll.append(10)
ll.append(20)
ll.append(30)

# Traverse the list
ll.traverse()  # Output: 10 -> 20 -> 30 -> None

# Delete a node
ll.delete(20)
ll.traverse()  # Output: 10 -> 30 -> None
```

---

3. Operations: Insertion, Deletion, Traversal

Insertion:

- **At the beginning**: Insert a new node at the head of the list.
- **At the end**: Insert a new node at the tail (last node) of the list.
- **At a specific position**: Insert a new node at a given position (after a specific node).

python

```
# Insertion at the beginning
def insert_at_beginning(self, data):
    new_node = Node(data)
    new_node.next = self.head  # Point the new node to the current head
    self.head = new_node  # Make the new node the head
```

Deletion:

- **From the beginning**: Remove the head node.
- **From the end**: Traverse to the last node and remove the previous node's next pointer.
- **By value**: Remove the node that contains a specific value.

python

```python
# Deletion at the beginning
def delete_at_beginning(self):
    if self.head:
        self.head = self.head.next  # Move the head pointer to the next node
```

Traversal:

Traversal is the process of visiting each node in the list and performing an operation (e.g., printing the data). In a singly linked list, we traverse starting from the head and move through each node by following the next pointer.

python

```python
# Traversal of the list
def traverse(self):
    current = self.head
    while current:
        print(current.data, end=" -> ")
        current = current.next
    print("None")
```

4. Types of Linked Lists

- **Singly Linked List**:
  - Each node points to the next node in the list.
  - Simple and efficient but can only be traversed in one direction.

- **Doubly Linked List**:
  - Each node has two pointers: one to the next node and one to the previous node. This allows traversal in both directions.
  - More memory consumption due to the additional pointer, but provides more flexibility for insertion and deletion.

python

```
class DoublyNode:
    def __init__(self, data):
        self.data = data
        self.next = None
        self.prev = None  # Additional pointer to the previous node
```

- **Circular Linked List**:
  - The last node points back to the first node, forming a circle.

o Can be either singly or doubly circular. Useful in scenarios like round-robin scheduling.

---

5. Use Cases of Linked Lists

- **Dynamic Memory Allocation**: Linked lists allow for dynamic memory allocation because they can grow and shrink in size at runtime. This is particularly useful in situations where you don't know in advance how many elements will be needed.

- **Linked List as Queues**: Linked lists can be used to implement a **queue** (FIFO structure) by using the head and tail pointers. Enqueue operations can be done at the tail (rear), and dequeue operations can be done at the head (front).

python

```python
class QueueUsingLinkedList:
    def __init__(self):
        self.head = None
        self.tail = None

    def enqueue(self, data):
        new_node = Node(data)
        if self.tail:
```

```
    self.tail.next = new_node
  self.tail = new_node
  if not self.head:
    self.head = new_node

def dequeue(self):
  if self.head:
    front = self.head
    self.head = self.head.next
    return front.data
  return None
```

Linked lists are powerful and versatile data structures that allow efficient insertion and deletion of elements, making them ideal for scenarios where frequent modifications to data are needed. They are different from arrays in that they do not require contiguous memory allocation, providing greater flexibility in dynamic memory allocation.

In this chapter, we've covered:

- The basic operations on linked lists (insertion, deletion, and traversal).
- The differences between singly, doubly, and circular linked lists.
- Real-world use cases, including dynamic memory management and implementing queues.

As you progress through the book, we will delve deeper into more advanced data structures and algorithms, building on the foundational concepts introduced in this chapter. In the next chapter, we will explore **Hash Tables**, another powerful data structure often used for fast lookups and efficient data storage.

CHAPTER 8: TREES: AN INTRODUCTION

In this chapter, we will explore **trees**, which are a fundamental non-linear data structure used to represent hierarchical relationships. Trees are particularly useful in scenarios where you need to model parent-child relationships, such as representing files in a file system, storing data in databases, or organizing objects in a hierarchy.

Unlike linear data structures like arrays and linked lists, **trees** allow for more efficient search, insertion, and deletion operations, especially when the data is organized in a hierarchical or sorted manner. Understanding trees is crucial for mastering algorithms that manipulate hierarchical data efficiently.

---

1. What is a Tree Data Structure?

A **tree** is a hierarchical data structure that consists of a collection of nodes, where:

- **Each node** stores a value (or data) and has references (or links) to child nodes.
- The **topmost node** in the tree is called the **root**.
- A **leaf node** is a node that has no children.
- The **edges** represent connections between nodes.

In contrast to linear data structures (like arrays or linked lists), trees are **non-linear** and allow data to be arranged in multiple levels, which makes them perfect for representing hierarchies or classifications.

Key Terms:

- **Node**: An element of the tree, consisting of data and references (or pointers) to child nodes.
- **Root**: The topmost node in a tree, from which all other nodes descend.
- **Leaf**: A node with no children (i.e., an endpoint).
- **Edge**: A link or reference between two nodes in the tree.
- **Height**: The height of a node is the length of the longest path from the node to a leaf. The height of the tree is the height of its root.
- **Depth**: The depth of a node is the number of edges from the root to the node.

---

2. Types of Trees

There are various types of trees, each suited for different types of applications. Let's explore some of the most common tree structures:

Binary Tree:

A **binary tree** is a tree in which each node has at most two children (commonly referred to as **left** and **right** children). Binary trees are foundational in tree-based algorithms and are the building blocks for many more advanced data structures.

python

```
class TreeNode:
```

```python
def __init__(self, data):
    self.data = data
    self.left = None  # Left child
    self.right = None  # Right child
```

Binary Search Tree (BST):

A **binary search tree** is a type of binary tree where the nodes are arranged in a specific order:

- The left child of a node contains a value less than the parent node.

- The right child contains a value greater than the parent node.

This ordering allows efficient searching, insertion, and deletion operations, typically in O(log n) time if the tree is balanced.

python

```python
class BST:
    def __init__(self):
        self.root = None

    def insert(self, data):
        if not self.root:
            self.root = TreeNode(data)
        else:
            self._insert_recursive(self.root, data)

    def _insert_recursive(self, node, data):
```

```
    if data < node.data:
        if node.left is None:
            node.left = TreeNode(data)
        else:
            self._insert_recursive(node.left, data)
    else:
        if node.right is None:
            node.right = TreeNode(data)
        else:
            self._insert_recursive(node.right, data)


def search(self, data):
    return self._search_recursive(self.root, data)


def _search_recursive(self, node, data):
    if node is None or node.data == data:
        return node
    elif data < node.data:
        return self._search_recursive(node.left, data)
    else:
        return self._search_recursive(node.right, data)
```

AVL Tree:

An **AVL tree** is a self-balancing binary search tree, meaning that it automatically maintains its balance after insertions and deletions. The key feature of an AVL tree is that the difference between the heights of the left and right subtrees (called the **balance factor**) of any node is at most 1. If the balance factor goes beyond this limit, the tree rebalances itself.

python

An AVL tree would require additional logic for rotations to ensure balancing.

Other Types of Trees:

- **Heap**: A special tree-based structure used to implement priority queues.
- **Trie**: A tree used to store strings in a way that allows efficient searching and prefix matching.
- **B-tree**: A balanced tree commonly used in databases for searching, inserting, and deleting data.

---

3. Implementing Trees in Python

Now that we understand the types of trees, let's see how we can implement a **Binary Search Tree (BST)** in Python.

Creating a Binary Search Tree:

Here's a basic implementation of a Binary Search Tree with **insert** and **search** operations:

python

```
class TreeNode:
    def __init__(self, data):
        self.data = data
        self.left = None
        self.right = None
```

```python
class BinarySearchTree:
    def __init__(self):
        self.root = None

    def insert(self, data):
        new_node = TreeNode(data)
        if not self.root:
            self.root = new_node
        else:
            self._insert(self.root, new_node)

    def _insert(self, current, new_node):
        if new_node.data < current.data:
            if current.left is None:
                current.left = new_node
            else:
                self._insert(current.left, new_node)
        else:
            if current.right is None:
                current.right = new_node
            else:
                self._insert(current.right, new_node)

    def search(self, data):
        return self._search(self.root, data)

    def _search(self, current, data):
        if current is None or current.data == data:
            return current
```

```
    if data < current.data:
        return self._search(current.left, data)
    else:
        return self._search(current.right, data)


# Example Usage:
bst = BinarySearchTree()
bst.insert(10)
bst.insert(20)
bst.insert(5)
bst.insert(15)


found_node = bst.search(15)
if found_node:
    print(f"Node found with value: {found_node.data}")
else:
    print("Node not found.")
```

This simple Binary Search Tree allows us to insert nodes while maintaining the tree's sorted property and search for a node efficiently.

4. Real-World Applications of Trees

Trees are used in many real-world applications where data needs to be stored and retrieved efficiently in a hierarchical manner. Here are a few examples:

1. File Systems:

In file systems, directories and files are organized in a tree structure. The root node represents the file system's root directory, and each directory or file is a node. The **directory structure** is a perfect example of a tree, where each directory may contain files or other directories (subdirectories).

2. Database Indexing:

In databases, tree structures like **B-trees** are used to index data, making it faster to search for records in large datasets. Trees provide efficient ways to keep records sorted and allow quick lookups, insertions, and deletions.

3. Decision Trees:

In machine learning, **decision trees** are used for classification tasks. A decision tree is a tree where each internal node represents a decision based on a feature, and each leaf node represents a class label.

4. Hierarchical Data Representation:

Trees are used in various applications where data has a hierarchical relationship, such as representing family trees, organizational charts, and taxonomies.

In this chapter, we have learned about **trees**, a versatile non-linear data structure that allows us to model hierarchical relationships. We covered:

- The basic terminology associated with trees (nodes, edges, root, leaves, etc.).
- Various types of trees like **binary trees**, **binary search trees (BST)**, and **AVL trees**.
- How to implement and manipulate binary trees in Python, including insertion and search operations.
- Real-world applications of trees in file systems, databases, and more.

As we progress through this book, we will build on this knowledge and explore more advanced tree structures and algorithms, such as **heap** trees and **trie** trees, which have specialized uses in different domains of computer science.

In the next chapter, we will dive deeper into **binary trees**, covering advanced topics like tree traversal algorithms and more complex tree operations.

CHAPTER 9: BINARY TREES AND BINARY SEARCH TREES

In this chapter, we will focus on **Binary Trees (BT)** and **Binary Search Trees (BST)**, which are crucial data structures for efficiently storing and searching data in a hierarchical manner. We will cover their structure, properties, operations, and practical uses. Binary search trees, in particular, are optimized for fast search, insertion, and deletion operations, which makes them an essential tool for many software systems, including databases and file systems.

---

1. Structure and Properties of Binary Trees

A **binary tree** is a tree data structure where each node has at most two children, which are referred to as the **left** and **right** child nodes. These child nodes are connected to the parent node via edges, creating a hierarchical structure.

Properties of Binary Trees:

- Each node contains:
  - A **data** field that holds the node's value.
  - A **left** child, which is another node in the tree (or **None** if it has no left child).
  - A **right** child, which is another node in the tree (or **None** if it has no right child).
- **Height of the tree**: The height of a binary tree is the length of the longest path from the root node to any leaf node. A tree with a height of h has at most $2^h - 1$ nodes.
- **Depth of a node**: The depth of a node is the number of edges from the root to the node.

Example:

Here is a simple illustration of a binary tree:

markdown

```
    10
   / \
  5   20
 /\  /\
3  8 15 30
```

In this tree:

- The **root node** is 10.
- The **left child** of 10 is 5, and the **right child** is 20.
- The **leaf nodes** (nodes with no children) are 3, 8, 15, and 30.

---

2. Operations on Binary Trees

Insertion:

Insertion in a binary tree is generally done in a manner where new nodes are added to the tree following certain rules, depending on the application. In general, we add new nodes to the left or right of existing nodes based on some condition (e.g., the value of the new node).

python

```python
class TreeNode:
    def __init__(self, data):
```

```python
        self.data = data
        self.left = None
        self.right = None

class BinaryTree:
    def __init__(self):
        self.root = None

    def insert(self, data):
        new_node = TreeNode(data)
        if self.root is None:
            self.root = new_node
        else:
            self._insert(self.root, new_node)

    def _insert(self, node, new_node):
        if new_node.data < node.data:
            if node.left is None:
                node.left = new_node
            else:
                self._insert(node.left, new_node)
        else:
            if node.right is None:
                node.right = new_node
            else:
                self._insert(node.right, new_node)

# Example usage
bt = BinaryTree()
bt.insert(10)
```

bt.insert(5)

bt.insert(20)

Traversal is the process of visiting each node in a tree in a specific order. In binary trees, we typically use three types of traversals:

- **Pre-order**: Visit the root, traverse the left subtree, then the right subtree.
- **In-order**: Traverse the left subtree, visit the root, then the right subtree.
- **Post-order**: Traverse the left subtree, the right subtree, then visit the root.

Here is how we can implement these traversals:

python

```python
class BinaryTree:
    def __init__(self):
        self.root = None

    def pre_order(self, node):
        if node:
            print(node.data, end=" ")
            self.pre_order(node.left)
            self.pre_order(node.right)

    def in_order(self, node):
        if node:
```

```
        self.in_order(node.left)
        print(node.data, end=" ")
        self.in_order(node.right)

    def post_order(self, node):
        if node:
            self.post_order(node.left)
            self.post_order(node.right)
            print(node.data, end=" ")


# Example usage
bt = BinaryTree()
bt.insert(10)
bt.insert(5)
bt.insert(20)
print("Pre-order traversal:")
bt.pre_order(bt.root)  # Output: 10 5 20
```

Deletion:

In binary trees, deletion is more complex than insertion because we need to maintain the tree's structure. Deleting a node can involve three main cases:

1. **Node with no children**: Simply remove the node.
2. **Node with one child**: Remove the node and link its parent to its only child.
3. **Node with two children**: Find the in-order successor (or predecessor) of the node, replace the node with that successor, and then delete the successor node.

3. Introduction to Binary Search Trees (BST)

A **binary search tree (BST)** is a type of binary tree where the nodes are arranged in a specific order:

- For each node, all nodes in its left subtree contain values less than the node's value.
- All nodes in its right subtree contain values greater than the node's value.

This ordering property allows for efficient searching, insertion, and deletion operations, as we can always compare the value we're looking for with the node's value and decide whether to move left or right in the tree.

Example:

Consider the following **Binary Search Tree**:

markdown

```
    10
   / \
  5   20
 /\  /\
3  8 15 30
```

- All nodes in the left subtree of 10 (i.e., 5, 3, and 8) are smaller than 10.

- All nodes in the right subtree of 10 (i.e., 20, 15, 30) are larger than 10.

BST Operations:

- **Insertion**: Insert a node by traversing from the root node, deciding whether to move left or right based on the node's value until we find an appropriate empty position.
- **Search**: Searching in a BST is similar to insertion. You compare the value with the current node's value and move left or right, depending on whether the value is smaller or larger.

python

```python
class BinarySearchTree:
    def __init__(self):
        self.root = None

    def insert(self, data):
        new_node = TreeNode(data)
        if not self.root:
            self.root = new_node
        else:
            self._insert(self.root, new_node)

    def _insert(self, node, new_node):
        if new_node.data < node.data:
            if node.left is None:
```

```
            node.left = new_node
        else:
            self._insert(node.left, new_node)
    else:
        if node.right is None:
            node.right = new_node
        else:
            self._insert(node.right, new_node)

def search(self, data):
    return self._search(self.root, data)

def _search(self, node, data):
    if node is None or node.data == data:
        return node
    elif data < node.data:
        return self._search(node.left, data)
    else:
        return self._search(node.right, data)


# Example usage
bst = BinarySearchTree()
bst.insert(10)
bst.insert(5)
bst.insert(20)
bst.insert(15)
found_node = bst.search(15)
if found_node:
    print(f"Node found with value: {found_node.data}")  # Output: Node found
with value: 15
```

4. Searching in Binary Search Trees

The searching algorithm in a **BST** is quite efficient. Given the sorted nature of the tree, we can eliminate half of the tree at each step:

- If the target value is less than the current node's value, move to the left subtree.
- If the target value is greater than the current node's value, move to the right subtree.
- This allows for **O(log n)** search time in a balanced BST, which is much faster than searching through a linear list or array.

5. Balancing Binary Search Trees

Over time, as you insert and delete nodes from a BST, it may become **unbalanced**, meaning that one side of the tree becomes deeper than the other. This imbalance can degrade the performance of the tree, turning search and insertion into **O(n)** operations in the worst case.

To ensure that the BST remains efficient, **self-balancing BSTs** like **AVL trees** and **Red-Black trees** are used. These trees automatically balance themselves after every insertion or deletion operation, maintaining a height difference of at most 1 between the left and right subtrees, thus ensuring **O(log n)** operations.

6. Real-World Applications of Binary Search Trees

Binary Search Trees and their variations (like AVL trees and Red-Black trees) are used in several real-world applications, including:

- **Database indexing**: Efficient search, insertion, and deletion operations for managing large datasets.
- **File systems**: Some file systems use trees to manage directories and files hierarchically.
- **Autocompletion**: Implementing word suggestions in search engines and applications.
- **Priority queues**: Used in scheduling algorithms, where the highest-priority tasks are always at the root of the tree.

In this chapter, we explored **binary trees** and **binary search trees (BST)**, focusing on their structure, properties, and key operations. We discussed how BSTs are particularly useful for efficient search, insertion, and deletion operations due to their ordering properties. Additionally, we covered traversal techniques (pre-order, in-order, post-order), which are fundamental for visiting all the nodes in the tree.

In the next chapter, we will dive deeper into more complex tree structures, including **AVL trees** and **Red-Black trees**, which are designed to maintain balanced binary search trees for more consistent performance.

CHAPTER 10: AVL TREES

In this chapter, we will dive into **AVL trees**, which are a type of **self-balancing binary search tree (BST)**. AVL trees automatically adjust their structure to ensure that their height remains balanced, thus maintaining optimal search times even as elements are added or removed. This is achieved through **rotations** and **balancing operations**, making them crucial in applications where search efficiency is paramount, such as databases, filesystems, and other performance-critical systems.

---

1. Understanding Self-Balancing Binary Search Trees

A **self-balancing binary search tree** (BST) is a tree that automatically keeps its height balanced as elements are inserted and deleted. The primary goal of a self-balancing tree is to ensure that the tree does not become skewed, which would result in degraded performance (i.e., turning into a linked list).

The height of a tree is defined as the number of edges on the longest path from the root node to any leaf node. For an unbalanced tree, operations such as search, insertion, and deletion could take linear time (O(n)), whereas a balanced tree ensures that these operations are logarithmic (O(log n)).

In an **AVL tree**, the difference in height between the left and right subtrees of any node is maintained to be no more than **1**. If this condition is violated, the tree performs **rotations** to restore balance.

---

2. The Need for Balanced Trees in Optimizing Search Time

The primary advantage of a balanced tree is the **guaranteed logarithmic search time**. Without balancing, a binary search tree could degenerate into a list (i.e., all nodes are on one side), resulting in a time complexity of O(n) for search operations. This is highly inefficient, especially when dealing with large datasets.

In an AVL tree, balancing ensures that:

- The height of the tree remains in the order of log(n) after each insertion or deletion.
- All search operations, insertion, and deletion are efficient, with a worst-case time complexity of O(log n).

Thus, AVL trees are particularly useful in scenarios where maintaining fast lookups, insertions, and deletions is crucial, such as in databases, caches, and high-performance indexing systems.

---

3. Rotations and Balancing Operations

Rotations are the key mechanism behind maintaining the balance in an AVL tree. When the height difference between the left and right subtrees (also called the **balance factor**) of a node becomes greater than 1 or less than -1, a rotation is performed to restore balance.

There are four types of rotations in AVL trees:

1. **Left Rotation (LL Rotation)**: This occurs when the left subtree of the left child of a node is too tall (i.e., the

balance factor of the left child is greater than 1). A left rotation helps to reduce the height of the left subtree.

Steps:

- o The node becomes the left child of its right child.
- o The right child's left subtree becomes the right subtree of the node.

Illustration:

lua

```
   30                20
   /                / \
   20     -->      10  30
  / \
 10  25
```

2. **Right Rotation (RR Rotation)**: This occurs when the right subtree of the right child of a node is too tall (i.e., the balance factor of the right child is less than -1). A right rotation helps to reduce the height of the right subtree.

Steps:

- o The node becomes the right child of its left child.
- o The left child's right subtree becomes the left subtree of the node.

Illustration:

lua

```
10                 20
  \              /  \
  20    -->    10   30
    \
    30
```

3. **Left-Right Rotation (LR Rotation)**: This occurs when the right child of the left subtree of a node is too tall. It is a combination of a **left rotation** followed by a **right rotation**.

Steps:

- First, perform a left rotation on the left child.
- Then, perform a right rotation on the node.

Illustration:

mathematica

```
  30                30                 20
 /                 /                  /  \
10    --> Left Rotate --> 20   --> Right Rotate --> 10   30
  \
  20
```

4. **Right-Left Rotation (RL Rotation)**: This occurs when the left child of the right subtree of a node is too tall. It is a combination of a **right rotation** followed by a **left rotation**.

Steps:

- ○ First, perform a right rotation on the right child.
- ○ Then, perform a left rotation on the node.

Illustration:

mathematica

```
10                10                20
  \                 \              /  \
   30   --> Right Rotate --> 20  --> Left Rotate --> 10  30
  /                 /
20                30
```

---

4. Implementing AVL Trees in Python

To implement an AVL tree in Python, we will need a **TreeNode** class to represent each node and an **AVLTree** class to handle insertions, deletions, rotations, and balancing.

TreeNode Class:

python

```
class TreeNode:
    def __init__(self, key):
```

```python
        self.key = key
        self.left = None
        self.right = None
        self.height = 1  # Height of node
```

AVLTree Class:

python

```python
class AVLTree:
    def __init__(self):
        self.root = None

    def insert(self, root, key):
        if not root:
            return TreeNode(key)

        if key < root.key:
            root.left = self.insert(root.left, key)
        else:
            root.right = self.insert(root.right, key)

        root.height = 1 + max(self.getHeight(root.left), self.getHeight(root.right))

        balance = self.getBalance(root)

        # Left Left Case
        if balance > 1 and key < root.left.key:
            return self.rightRotate(root)

        # Right Right Case
        if balance < -1 and key > root.right.key:
```

```python
        return self.leftRotate(root)

    # Left Right Case
    if balance > 1 and key > root.left.key:
        root.left = self.leftRotate(root.left)
        return self.rightRotate(root)

    # Right Left Case
    if balance < -1 and key < root.right.key:
        root.right = self.rightRotate(root.right)
        return self.leftRotate(root)

    return root

def leftRotate(self, z):
    y = z.right
    T2 = y.left

    # Perform rotation
    y.left = z
    z.right = T2

    # Update heights
    z.height = max(self.getHeight(z.left), self.getHeight(z.right)) + 1
    y.height = max(self.getHeight(y.left), self.getHeight(y.right)) + 1

    return y

def rightRotate(self, z):
    y = z.left
```

```python
        T3 = y.right

        # Perform rotation
        y.right = z
        z.left = T3

        # Update heights
        z.height = max(self.getHeight(z.left), self.getHeight(z.right)) + 1
        y.height = max(self.getHeight(y.left), self.getHeight(y.right)) + 1

        return y

    def getHeight(self, root):
        if not root:
            return 0
        return root.height

    def getBalance(self, root):
        if not root:
            return 0
        return self.getHeight(root.left) - self.getHeight(root.right)

    def preOrder(self, root):
        if not root:
            return
        print(root.key, end=" ")
        self.preOrder(root.left)
        self.preOrder(root.right)

# Example usage
```

```
avl_tree = AVLTree()
root = None
keys = [20, 30, 10, 5, 15, 25]

for key in keys:
    root = avl_tree.insert(root, key)

print("Pre-order traversal of the AVL tree:")
avl_tree.preOrder(root)
```

Explanation:

- The insert() function inserts a key into the AVL tree, balancing the tree if necessary by performing rotations.
- The leftRotate() and rightRotate() functions implement the two main types of rotations that help restore balance.
- The getHeight() function calculates the height of a node.
- The getBalance() function calculates the balance factor, which is the difference between the heights of the left and right subtrees.

---

5. Real-World Applications of AVL Trees

AVL trees are widely used in scenarios where fast search and update operations are essential. Some of the key real-world applications include:

- **Databases**: AVL trees are often used to index large datasets to speed up search operations, enabling efficient querying of data.

- **Filesystems**: Many file systems use AVL trees to manage files and directories, ensuring quick access to files in large directories.

- **Memory Management**: AVL trees are used in operating systems for managing memory blocks, as they allow for quick allocation and deallocation.

- **Networking**: AVL trees can be used in routing algorithms to maintain efficient paths for data transmission.

In this chapter, we introduced **AVL trees**, a type of self-balancing binary search tree. We covered the importance of balancing for optimizing search times and explored key balancing operations (rotations). We also implemented an AVL tree in Python and examined real-world applications that benefit from its efficiency.

In the next chapter, we will explore **Red-Black Trees**, another self-balancing binary search tree that provides a different approach to balancing and is commonly used in practical applications like the implementation of associative containers in C++.

CHAPTER 11: HEAPS AND PRIORITY QUEUES

In this chapter, we will explore **heaps**, a specialized tree-based data structure used to manage a dynamic set of elements where each element can be efficiently accessed based on priority. Heaps are often used in **priority queues**, which are central to many scheduling and optimization algorithms. We'll cover both **min-heaps** and **max-heaps**, demonstrate their implementation in

DATA STRUCTURES IN PYTHON

Python using the heapq module, and explore practical applications, including task scheduling.

---

1. Introduction to Heaps: Min-Heap vs Max-Heap

A **heap** is a binary tree with two main properties:

- **Shape Property**: A heap is a complete binary tree, meaning it is perfectly balanced except possibly for the last level, which is filled from left to right.
- **Heap Property**: The key at each node follows a specific order relative to its children.

There are two types of heaps:

- **Min-Heap**: In a min-heap, the key at each node is smaller than or equal to the keys of its children. This ensures that the minimum element is always at the root. A min-heap is useful when you need to access the smallest element quickly.

  Example: In a min-heap, the smallest element is at the root, and every parent node is smaller than its children.

- **Max-Heap**: In a max-heap, the key at each node is greater than or equal to the keys of its children. This ensures that the maximum element is always at the root. A max-heap is used when the largest element needs to be accessed quickly.

Example: In a max-heap, the largest element is at the root, and every parent node is greater than its children.

---

2. Implementing Heaps in Python Using the *heapq* Module

Python's heapq module provides a straightforward implementation of **min-heaps**, and while it doesn't explicitly support max-heaps, you can easily simulate a max-heap by negating the values stored in the heap.

Min-Heap Example (Default Behavior):

python

```
import heapq

# Create an empty heap (list)
heap = []

# Insert elements into the heap
heapq.heappush(heap, 20)
heapq.heappush(heap, 15)
heapq.heappush(heap, 30)
heapq.heappush(heap, 10)

# View the heap (smallest element is at the root)
print("Min-Heap:", heap)  # [10, 15, 30, 20]
```

```python
# Pop the smallest element (root)
smallest = heapq.heappop(heap)
print("Smallest Element:", smallest)  # 10

# View the heap after popping
print("Min-Heap after pop:", heap)  # [15, 20, 30]
```

In this example:

- heapq.heappush(heap, element) inserts an element into the heap while maintaining the heap property.
- heapq.heappop(heap) removes and returns the smallest element, which is always the root of the min-heap.

Max-Heap Simulation:

To simulate a max-heap, you can negate the values before pushing them into the heap. This way, the largest value will become the smallest (most negative) value in the heap, and popping from the heap will give the largest element.

python

```python
import heapq

# Create an empty heap for max-heap (using negation)
max_heap = []

# Insert elements into the heap (negate to simulate max-heap)
heapq.heappush(max_heap, -20)
```

```
heapq.heappush(max_heap, -15)
heapq.heappush(max_heap, -30)
heapq.heappush(max_heap, -10)

# View the max-heap (note the negative values)
print("Max-Heap:", [-x for x in max_heap])  # [30, 20, 15, 10]

# Pop the largest element (root)
largest = -heapq.heappop(max_heap)
print("Largest Element:", largest)  # 30

# View the heap after popping
print("Max-Heap after pop:", [-x for x in max_heap])  # [20, 15, 10]
```

Here, -x is used to simulate a max-heap, where heapq.heappop() returns the most negative value, and we negate it back to get the actual largest value.

---

3. Operations: Insertion, Deletion, Heapify

Insertion (Push Operation):

- When inserting an element into a heap, the heap property must be maintained.
- **Insertion Process**:
    1. Add the element to the end of the tree (or list).
    2. "Bubble up" the element to restore the heap property if needed.

In Python, the heapq.heappush() function performs this process.

Deletion (Pop Operation):

- Deletion from a heap involves removing the root element (the smallest in a min-heap or the largest in a max-heap).
- **Deletion Process**:
    1. Remove the root element.
    2. Replace the root with the last element in the tree.
    3. "Bubble down" the element to restore the heap property.

The heapq.heappop() function handles this process.

Heapify:

- The **heapify** process ensures that a list of elements satisfies the heap property. This can be done in-place using the heapq.heapify() function.

Example:

python

import heapq

# Create an unsorted list of elements
unsorted_list = [20, 15, 30, 10]

```
# Heapify the list
heapq.heapify(unsorted_list)
```

```
# The list is now a valid min-heap
print("Heapified List:", unsorted_list)  # [10, 15, 30, 20]
```

This function converts an unsorted list into a heap efficiently, in O(n) time.

---

4. Priority Queues and Their Applications

A **priority queue** is a data structure where each element is assigned a priority, and elements are dequeued in order of their priority, not in the order they were enqueued. A priority queue is often implemented using a heap because it allows efficient retrieval of the element with the highest (or lowest) priority.

- **Priority Queue Operations**:
    - **Insertion**: Insert an element with a priority.
    - **Dequeue**: Retrieve and remove the element with the highest priority.
    - **Peek**: View the element with the highest priority without removing it.

Priority queues are commonly used in algorithms like:

- **Dijkstra's Algorithm** for shortest path calculation
- **Huffman Coding** for data compression

- **Task Scheduling** where tasks are processed based on their priority.

Task Scheduling Example:

Consider a task scheduling system where tasks are processed based on their priority. We can use a **priority queue** (min-heap) to manage tasks with different priorities.

python

```
import heapq

# Define tasks with (priority, task_name) tuples
tasks = [(3, 'Write Report'), (1, 'Check Email'), (2, 'Meeting with Boss')]

# Create an empty priority queue (min-heap)
priority_queue = []

# Insert tasks into the priority queue
for task in tasks:
    heapq.heappush(priority_queue, task)

# Process tasks based on priority
while priority_queue:
    priority, task = heapq.heappop(priority_queue)
    print(f'Processing task: {task} with priority {priority}")
```

Output:

sql

Processing task: Check Email with priority 1

Processing task: Meeting with Boss with priority 2

Processing task: Write Report with priority 3

In this example:

- Tasks are inserted into the priority queue along with their priorities.
- The task with the lowest priority value is processed first because we are using a **min-heap**.

---

5. Practical Example: Task Scheduling

A **task scheduler** is a real-world example where priority queues are essential. Imagine you are building a task management system for a cloud-based application where multiple tasks (like file uploads, data processing, etc.) need to be processed based on their urgency.

Using a priority queue, you can efficiently manage and schedule tasks. Each task has a **priority**, and the scheduler ensures that the most urgent tasks are processed first, allowing the system to handle critical tasks promptly.

In this case, a priority queue implemented using a min-heap or max-heap will provide O(log n) time complexity for each insertion and removal, making it highly efficient for real-time systems.

In this chapter, we introduced **heaps** and their importance in implementing **priority queues**. We explored both **min-heaps** and **max-heaps**, demonstrated how to implement them in Python using the heapq module, and examined their real-world applications, particularly in task scheduling and algorithms like Dijkstra's shortest path.

In the next chapter, we will explore **Hash Tables** (also known as **Hash Maps**) and their significance in providing fast lookups, insertions, and deletions.

CHAPTER 12: TRIE (PREFIX TREE)

In this chapter, we will delve into the **Trie** (also known as a **Prefix Tree**), a specialized tree-based data structure used for storing strings in a way that allows efficient **prefix-based search operations**. Tries are particularly useful when we need to store and query large sets of strings, such as in **autocomplete systems, spell checkers**, or **dictionary lookups**.

A **Trie** is a tree-like structure where each node represents a single character in a string, and paths down the tree represent prefixes of words. This structure allows for **fast prefix matching** and is particularly effective when we need to search for strings that share common prefixes.

---

1. Introduction to Trie Data Structure

A **Trie** is a tree that stores strings in a way that enables efficient prefix-based searching. It is a **multi-way tree** where each node typically represents a character of a string. Unlike traditional trees, which store entire strings in each node, a Trie stores one character per node and relies on the path down the tree to represent the string.

The **key properties** of a Trie are:

- **Nodes represent characters**: Each node stores a single character, and edges between nodes represent the sequence of characters in a string.
- **Prefix-based search**: Tries enable searching for strings by their prefixes, making them suitable for tasks like autocomplete, spell checking, and dictionary lookup.

- **Efficient search**: Searching for strings in a Trie is much faster than a linear search, particularly when there are many strings that share common prefixes.

Basic Terminology:

- **Root Node**: The starting point of the Trie, which doesn't store any characters.
- **Child Nodes**: Each node in the Trie has a set of child nodes representing the next character in the string.
- **End-of-Word Marker**: A special marker (often a boolean flag) to indicate whether a node marks the end of a valid string in the Trie.

---

2. Implementing a Trie in Python

To implement a Trie in Python, we need to define two components:

1. A **TrieNode** class to represent the individual nodes.
2. A **Trie** class to manage the root node and implement insert and search operations.

TrieNode Class

Each node in the Trie stores:

- A dictionary of **children** (representing the next characters in the string).

- A **boolean flag** indicating if the node marks the end of a word.

python

```python
class TrieNode:
    def __init__(self):
        self.children = {}
        self.is_end_of_word = False
```

Trie Class

The Trie class will manage the root node and provide methods to insert and search strings.

python

```python
class Trie:
    def __init__(self):
        self.root = TrieNode()

    # Insert a word into the Trie
    def insert(self, word):
        node = self.root
        for char in word:
            if char not in node.children:
                node.children[char] = TrieNode()
            node = node.children[char]
        node.is_end_of_word = True

    # Search for a word in the Trie
```

```python
def search(self, word):
    node = self.root
    for char in word:
        if char not in node.children:
            return False  # Word not found
        node = node.children[char]
    return node.is_end_of_word  # Check if it's a valid word


    # Search for words with a given prefix
    def starts_with(self, prefix):
        node = self.root
        for char in prefix:
            if char not in node.children:
                return False  # No such prefix
            node = node.children[char]
        return True  # Prefix exists
```

Example Usage:

python

```python
# Create a Trie instance
trie = Trie()


# Insert words into the Trie
trie.insert("apple")
trie.insert("app")
trie.insert("banana")


# Search for words
print(trie.search("apple"))  # True
print(trie.search("app"))    # True
```

```
print(trie.search("banana"))  # True
print(trie.search("bat"))     # False

# Search for prefix
print(trie.starts_with("ban"))  # True
print(trie.starts_with("bat"))  # False
```

In this example:

- The insert method adds words to the Trie.
- The search method checks if a specific word is present in the Trie.
- The starts_with method checks if a given prefix exists in the Trie.

---

3. Use Cases for Trie Data Structures

1. Dictionary Lookups: In a dictionary application, we need to check if a given word exists. A Trie allows us to efficiently perform this check. For example, if the user types "cat", the Trie can quickly find the word "cat" and also suggest related words like "catalog" or "cattle", based on shared prefixes.

2. Autocomplete Systems: Tries are widely used in **autocomplete** systems, such as those used by search engines or mobile keyboards. By storing a list of possible words in the Trie, an autocomplete system can suggest completions for the prefix typed by the user.

For example:

- If a user types "ap", the system might suggest "apple", "apricot", "applied", etc.
- The Trie structure allows quick retrieval of all words that share the "ap" prefix.

3. Spell Checkers: Spell checkers rely on efficient searching to detect if a word exists in a dictionary or to suggest similar words. The Trie allows for fast lookup of potentially misspelled words and suggests corrections based on similar prefixes.

4. IP Routing Tables: In computer networks, a Trie can be used for routing table lookups, where each node represents a prefix of an IP address. This structure helps in efficiently matching incoming packets to the correct route.

---

4. Time and Space Complexity Analysis
Time Complexity:

- **Insertion**: The time complexity for inserting a word is $O(m)$, where m is the length of the word. This is because we need to traverse each character in the word to insert it into the Trie.

- **Search**: Searching for a word takes $O(m)$ time, where m is the length of the word, as we traverse through each character in the Trie to match the word.
- **Prefix Search**: Searching for a prefix also takes $O(m)$ time, where m is the length of the prefix, as we need to traverse down the Trie to match the prefix.

Space Complexity:

- The space complexity of a Trie is $O(n * m)$, where n is the number of words and m is the average length of the words. This is because each node stores a single character and each word is represented by a path of nodes in the Trie.
- If there are many shared prefixes (e.g., "apple", "app", "apply"), the Trie saves space by reusing nodes for common prefixes.

Optimization Considerations:

- A Trie can become quite large if there are many unique strings with long prefixes. However, it provides fast search and insertion operations compared to other data structures like hash tables, particularly when there are many common prefixes.

In this chapter, we introduced the **Trie** (Prefix Tree) data structure, which is highly efficient for storing and searching strings, especially when prefix-based searches are common. We explored how to implement a Trie in Python and demonstrated its use in applications such as **autocomplete systems**, **spell checkers**, and **dictionary lookups**.

We also discussed the **time and space complexities** associated with Tries, highlighting their efficiency in terms of search time and their storage overhead due to the structure of the tree.

In the next chapter, we will explore **Hash Tables** (also known as **Hash Maps**), another powerful data structure used for efficient lookups, insertions, and deletions.

CHAPTER 13: INTRODUCTION TO GRAPHS

In this chapter, we will explore the fundamental data structure known as **graphs**, which are widely used in computer science and real-world applications such as social networks, maps, network routing, and recommendation systems. Understanding graphs is essential because they form the backbone of many algorithms in computer science, particularly those related to navigation, optimization, and connectivity.

1. What is a Graph and How is it Different from Trees?

A **graph** is a collection of **nodes** (also called **vertices**) and **edges** (also called **links**) that connect pairs of nodes. Unlike trees, which are a special type of graph, a general graph may have cycles and multiple connections between nodes, making it more flexible but also more complex to work with.

Key Differences Between Graphs and Trees:

- **Cycles**: A tree is a type of graph that **does not** contain cycles (i.e., there is exactly one path between any two nodes). In contrast, a general graph may have cycles (i.e., multiple paths can exist between nodes).
- **Connectivity**: In a tree, there is exactly one path between any two nodes, whereas, in a graph, there can be multiple paths between nodes.
- **Structure**: A tree has a hierarchical structure (rooted), while a graph can have any kind of structure, including cyclic, directed, or undirected.

2. *Types of Graphs*

There are different types of graphs, each suited for different types of problems:

a. Directed Graphs (Digraphs):

- In a **directed graph**, the edges have a direction, meaning that the edge from node **A** to node **B** is not the same as the edge from **B** to **A**. Directed edges are often represented by arrows.

- **Real-world examples**: Twitter follows, where one user can follow another, but the reverse is not necessarily true.

b. Undirected Graphs:

- In an **undirected graph**, the edges do not have any direction, meaning the edge between node **A** and node **B** is the same as the edge between **B** and **A**. These graphs are typically used to model mutual relationships.

- **Real-world examples**: Facebook friendships, where if **A** is friends with **B**, **B** is also friends with **A**.

c. Weighted Graphs:

- In a **weighted graph**, each edge has a weight or cost associated with it. These weights could represent distance, time, cost, or any other value that can be associated with the connection between two nodes.

- **Real-world examples**: Flight paths between cities, where the edges represent the distance or cost of travel between two airports.

d. Unweighted Graphs:

- In an **unweighted graph**, all edges are considered equal, i.e., there is no associated weight or cost. These graphs are typically used when the relationship between nodes is simple and does not require prioritization or cost consideration.

- **Real-world examples**: Social networks where connections are either present or absent, but not associated with a value.

3. Representing Graphs in Python

Graphs can be represented in different ways in memory, with two common representations being **adjacency lists** and **adjacency matrices**. Both representations have their own strengths and weaknesses, depending on the type of graph and the operations we need to perform.

a. Adjacency List:

- An **adjacency list** is an array or list where each index represents a node and stores a list of all the nodes connected to it. This representation is space-efficient for sparse graphs (graphs with few edges relative to the number of nodes).

- **Example**:

python

```
# Adjacency list representation
graph = {
    'A': ['B', 'C'],
    'B': ['A', 'D', 'E'],
    'C': ['A'],
    'D': ['B'],
    'E': ['B']
}
```

Here, node **A** is connected to nodes **B** and **C**, node **B** is connected to nodes **A**, **D**, and **E**, and so on.

b. Adjacency Matrix:

- An **adjacency matrix** is a 2D array where each element matrix[i][j] represents the presence (or absence) of an edge between nodes **i** and **j**. This representation is more suitable for dense graphs (graphs with many edges).
- **Example**:

python

```
# Adjacency matrix representation for an undirected graph
```

```
graph = [
    [0, 1, 1, 0, 0],  # A
    [1, 0, 0, 1, 1],  # B
    [1, 0, 0, 0, 0],  # C
    [0, 1, 0, 0, 0],  # D
    [0, 1, 0, 0, 0]   # E
]
```

In this example, the graph is represented as a 5x5 matrix, where a 1 represents the presence of an edge between nodes and a 0 represents the absence of an edge.

Note: Adjacency matrices are easier to use when checking if an edge exists between two nodes, as the check is done in constant time O(1). However, they consume more space (O(n^2)) than adjacency lists, especially for sparse graphs.

---

4. Graph Traversal Algorithms

Once we have represented a graph, we need to be able to **traverse** it, i.e., visit its nodes and edges. There are two fundamental graph traversal algorithms:

a. Breadth-First Search (BFS):

- BFS is a traversal algorithm that explores all the neighbors of a node before moving on to the next level. BFS explores the graph layer by layer, starting from a given source node.

- **Time complexity**: O(V + E), where **V** is the number of vertices (nodes) and **E** is the number of edges.

- **Real-world applications**: Finding the shortest path in an unweighted graph, networking applications like broadcasting messages.

BFS Implementation in Python:

python

```python
from collections import deque

def bfs(graph, start):
    visited = set()  # To keep track of visited nodes
    queue = deque([start])  # Use a queue for BFS

    while queue:
        node = queue.popleft()
        if node not in visited:
            print(node, end=" ")
            visited.add(node)
            for neighbor in graph[node]:
                if neighbor not in visited:
                    queue.append(neighbor)

# Example usage
graph = {
    'A': ['B', 'C'],
    'B': ['A', 'D', 'E'],
    'C': ['A'],
```

```
    'D': ['B'],
    'E': ['B']
}
```

bfs(graph, 'A')

b. Depth-First Search (DFS):

- DFS is a traversal algorithm that explores as far down a branch of the graph as possible before backtracking. DFS can be implemented using either recursion or an explicit stack.

- **Time complexity**: O(V + E), where **V** is the number of vertices and **E** is the number of edges.

- **Real-world applications**: Pathfinding, cycle detection, topological sorting.

DFS Implementation in Python (using recursion):

python

```python
def dfs(graph, node, visited=None):
    if visited is None:
        visited = set()
    visited.add(node)
    print(node, end=" ")

    for neighbor in graph[node]:
        if neighbor not in visited:
            dfs(graph, neighbor, visited)
```

```python
# Example usage
graph = {
  'A': ['B', 'C'],
  'B': ['A', 'D', 'E'],
  'C': ['A'],
  'D': ['B'],
  'E': ['B']
}

dfs(graph, 'A')
```

---

5. Real-World Applications of Graphs

Graphs are used to model many real-world scenarios, including:

- **Social Networks**: Users are represented as nodes, and friendships or relationships are edges. Graph algorithms can help with friend recommendations, mutual connections, etc.

- **Navigation Systems**: Cities or locations are nodes, and the roads or paths between them are edges. Graph traversal algorithms like BFS can help find the shortest path between two locations.

- **Recommendation Systems**: Graphs can model relationships between users and products, allowing for personalized recommendations based on user behavior.

In this chapter, we introduced **graphs** as a powerful data structure used to model relationships between entities. We explored the different types of graphs, such as **directed** and **undirected**, and discussed common representations, including **adjacency lists** and **adjacency matrices**.

We also covered two essential graph traversal algorithms—**Breadth-First Search (BFS)** and **Depth-First Search (DFS)**—with Python implementations. These algorithms form the foundation for many more advanced graph algorithms, including shortest path, network flow, and cycle detection.

In the next chapter, we will dive into **shortest path algorithms** and explore how graphs are used to find optimal paths in various contexts, from routing to social network analysis.

CHAPTER 14: GRAPH ALGORITHMS

In this chapter, we will explore some of the most fundamental and widely used graph algorithms, focusing on their applications and real-world utility. These algorithms allow us to solve complex problems related to **shortest paths**, **spanning trees**, and **graph ordering**, which are key to many modern technologies and systems. From **routing protocols** in computer networks to **social network analysis**, graph algorithms play a crucial role in optimizing processes, analyzing data, and improving performance.

1. Shortest Path Algorithms

One of the most common problems in graph theory is finding the **shortest path** between two nodes. This problem arises in various real-world scenarios such as GPS navigation, network routing, and pathfinding in games. We will discuss two primary algorithms for solving this problem: **Dijkstra's Algorithm** and **Bellman-Ford Algorithm**.

a. Dijkstra's Algorithm:

- **Dijkstra's Algorithm** is one of the most well-known algorithms for finding the shortest path from a single source node to all other nodes in a graph with **non-negative edge weights**.
- The algorithm works by iteratively selecting the node with the smallest tentative distance, then relaxing all its neighboring edges.

- **Time Complexity**: O(V^2) using a simple implementation, but it can be reduced to O((V + E) log V) using a priority queue (min-heap).

Steps of Dijkstra's Algorithm:

1. Initialize the distance of the source node to 0 and all other nodes to infinity.
2. Add the source node to the priority queue.
3. While the priority queue is not empty:
   - Extract the node with the smallest tentative distance.
   - Update the distances of its neighbors.
   - If the newly calculated distance is smaller than the current distance, update it.

Dijkstra's Algorithm in Python (using a priority queue):

python

```python
import heapq

def dijkstra(graph, start):
    # Initialize distances and the priority queue
    distances = {node: float('inf') for node in graph}
    distances[start] = 0
    priority_queue = [(0, start)]

    while priority_queue:
        current_distance, current_node = heapq.heappop(priority_queue)
```

```python
        if current_distance > distances[current_node]:
            continue

        for neighbor, weight in graph[current_node]:
            distance = current_distance + weight

            if distance < distances[neighbor]:
                distances[neighbor] = distance
                heapq.heappush(priority_queue, (distance, neighbor))

    return distances

# Example graph
graph = {
    'A': [('B', 1), ('C', 4)],
    'B': [('A', 1), ('C', 2), ('D', 5)],
    'C': [('A', 4), ('B', 2), ('D', 1)],
    'D': [('B', 5), ('C', 1)]
}

print(dijkstra(graph, 'A'))
```

b. Bellman-Ford Algorithm:

- **Bellman-Ford** is another algorithm for finding the shortest path from a single source node to all other nodes, but unlike Dijkstra's Algorithm, it can handle **negative edge weights**.

- However, it does not work efficiently when there are negative cycles (cycles where the sum of the edges is negative).
- **Time Complexity**: O(V * E), where **V** is the number of vertices and **E** is the number of edges.

Steps of Bellman-Ford Algorithm:

1. Initialize the distance to all nodes as infinity, except for the source node which is set to 0.
2. For each edge, update the distance of the destination node if a shorter path is found.
3. Repeat this process for **V-1** iterations (where **V** is the number of nodes).
4. After the **V-1** iterations, check for negative-weight cycles by trying to update the distances again.

Bellman-Ford Algorithm in Python:

python

```
def bellman_ford(graph, start):
    # Initialize distances
    distances = {node: float('inf') for node in graph}
    distances[start] = 0

    # Relax edges repeatedly
    for _ in range(len(graph) - 1):
```

```
    for node in graph:
        for neighbor, weight in graph[node]:
            if distances[node] + weight < distances[neighbor]:
                distances[neighbor] = distances[node] + weight

    # Check for negative-weight cycles
    for node in graph:
        for neighbor, weight in graph[node]:
            if distances[node] + weight < distances[neighbor]:
                print("Graph contains negative weight cycle")
                return None

    return distances

# Example graph
graph = {
    'A': [('B', 1), ('C', 4)],
    'B': [('A', 1), ('C', 2), ('D', 5)],
    'C': [('A', 4), ('B', 2), ('D', 1)],
    'D': [('B', 5), ('C', 1)]
}

print(bellman_ford(graph, 'A'))
```

---

2. Minimum Spanning Tree

A **Minimum Spanning Tree (MST)** is a subset of the edges of a connected, undirected graph that connects all the vertices together without any cycles and with the minimum possible total edge weight.

Two of the most famous algorithms for finding an MST are **Prim's Algorithm** and **Kruskal's Algorithm**.

a. Prim's Algorithm:

- **Prim's Algorithm** starts with a single node and expands the MST one edge at a time by adding the smallest possible edge that connects a new node to the existing MST.
- **Time Complexity**: O(E log V) when implemented with a priority queue.

Steps of Prim's Algorithm:

1. Initialize a priority queue with the starting node and its edges.
2. Repeatedly extract the minimum weight edge that connects a new node to the MST.
3. Add the edge to the MST and add the new node to the priority queue.

Prim's Algorithm in Python:

python

```python
import heapq

def prim(graph):
    mst = []  # To store the MST edges
    visited = set()  # To track visited nodes
```

```python
min_heap = [(0, 'A')]  # Start from node 'A'

while min_heap:
    weight, node = heapq.heappop(min_heap)

    if node not in visited:
        visited.add(node)
        mst.append((node, weight))

        for neighbor, edge_weight in graph[node]:
            if neighbor not in visited:
                heapq.heappush(min_heap, (edge_weight, neighbor))

return mst

# Example graph
graph = {
    'A': [('B', 1), ('C', 4)],
    'B': [('A', 1), ('C', 2), ('D', 5)],
    'C': [('A', 4), ('B', 2), ('D', 1)],
    'D': [('B', 5), ('C', 1)]
}

print(prim(graph))
```

b. Kruskal's Algorithm:

- **Kruskal's Algorithm** works by sorting all edges in the graph by weight and adding edges to the MST as long as they don't form a cycle. This is done using a **disjoint-set** data structure.

- **Time Complexity**: O(E log E), where **E** is the number of edges.

Steps of Kruskal's Algorithm:

1. Sort all the edges in increasing order of weight.
2. Use a disjoint-set (union-find) data structure to track the connected components.
3. Add edges to the MST, ensuring that adding an edge doesn't form a cycle.

---

3. Topological Sorting

Topological sorting is the process of ordering the vertices of a directed acyclic graph (DAG) in a linear sequence such that for every directed edge **uv**, vertex **u** comes before **v** in the ordering.

Topological sorting is used in scenarios such as:

- Task scheduling (where some tasks must be performed before others).
- Dependency resolution in software packages (e.g., determining the order in which to compile files).

Time Complexity: O(V + E) for both DFS-based and Kahn's algorithm-based approaches.

Topological Sorting in Python (using DFS):

python

```python
def topological_sort(graph):
    visited = set()
    stack = []

    def dfs(node):
        visited.add(node)
        for neighbor in graph[node]:
            if neighbor not in visited:
                dfs(neighbor)
        stack.append(node)

    for node in graph:
        if node not in visited:
            dfs(node)

    return stack[::-1]

# Example graph (DAG)
graph = {
    'A': ['B', 'C'],
    'B': ['D'],
    'C': ['D'],
    'D': []
}

print(topological_sort(graph))
```

4. Real-World Applications of Graph Algorithms

- **Social Networks**: In social media platforms like Facebook or Twitter, **shortest path algorithms** can be used to find the shortest path between two users, or **topological sorting** can help prioritize tasks in recommendation systems.

- **Routing Algorithms**: **Dijkstra's** and **Bellman-Ford** are commonly used in GPS navigation systems to find the shortest path between two locations. **Minimum Spanning Tree** algorithms like **Prim's** and **Kruskal's** are used in network design to minimize the cost of wiring.

- **Job Scheduling**: **Topological Sorting** is heavily used in job scheduling systems, where tasks have dependencies and must be executed in a specific order.

In this chapter, we covered several important graph algorithms, including **shortest path algorithms** like Dijkstra's and Bellman-Ford, and **minimum spanning tree algorithms** like Prim's and Kruskal's. We also explored **topological sorting** and its applications. Each of these algorithms serves a crucial role in solving real-world problems, from route planning to network optimization and task scheduling.

In the next chapter, we will delve deeper into **advanced graph algorithms**, exploring topics such as **network flow, cycle detection**, and **strongly connected components**, which form the foundation for even more complex graph-related problems.

CHAPTER 15: DIRECTED ACYCLIC GRAPHS (DAGS)

In this chapter, we will explore **Directed Acyclic Graphs (DAGs)**, a fundamental structure in graph theory that has wide applications in various domains such as **task scheduling**, **dependency resolution**, and **workflow management**. DAGs are essential for modeling systems where relationships between entities are directional but cannot form cycles, making them particularly useful for tasks that require ordered execution or hierarchical dependencies.

1. Understanding Directed Acyclic Graphs (DAGs)

A **Directed Acyclic Graph** is a graph that consists of **directed edges** and **nodes**, with two key properties:

- **Directed**: Each edge in the graph has a direction, indicating a one-way relationship between two nodes. In other words, the edges go from one node to another, but there is no bi-directional path.
- **Acyclic**: There are no cycles in the graph, meaning no node can be reached again by following the direction of edges starting from itself. This property ensures that the graph has a topological ordering where nodes can be sorted in a linear sequence.

Key Characteristics of a DAG:

- **Directionality**: The edges have a specific direction, representing relationships like "task A must precede task B."
- **Acyclicity**: A cycle-free structure ensures there are no circular dependencies or infinite loops.
- **Topological Order**: A DAG can always be topologically sorted, meaning its nodes can be arranged in such a way that for every directed edge $u \to v$, u appears before v in the ordering.

Visual Representation: Imagine a DAG where each node represents a task, and each directed edge represents a dependency between tasks. For example, task **A** must be completed before task **B** can start.

Here's an example of a simple DAG:

mathematica

```
A → B → D
↓   ↓
C → E
```

- Task **A** must be completed before tasks **B** and **C**.
- Task **B** must be completed before task **D**.
- Task **C** must be completed before task **E**.

2. Applications of DAGs in Task Scheduling and Dependency Resolution

Directed Acyclic Graphs are particularly useful in scenarios where tasks or operations depend on the completion of other tasks. The key applications of DAGs include:

a. Task Scheduling:

- In task scheduling systems, tasks often have dependencies. A DAG can model these dependencies, ensuring that each task is completed in the correct order. This is vital in fields like **distributed computing**, **project management**, and **CI/CD pipelines** where tasks depend on the completion of others.

- **Example**: A project management tool can use a DAG to represent a set of tasks. Tasks that are dependent on the completion of others will only be executed once their prerequisites are finished.

b. Dependency Resolution:

- In software development, **package managers** (like pip for Python, npm for JavaScript, or apt for Linux) use DAGs to manage dependencies between libraries or software packages. The goal is to ensure that all required dependencies are installed before a package is installed.

- **Example**: In npm, if package **A** depends on package **B**, package **B** must be installed first, which can be represented as a directed edge in a DAG.

c. Workflow Management:

- Workflow management systems (used in areas like data processing, ETL pipelines, and scientific computing) rely on DAGs to determine the order in which tasks should be executed. A DAG ensures that tasks that depend on others are executed in the correct sequence.

- **Example**: Apache **Airflow** is a popular open-source workflow automation tool that uses DAGs to model the sequence of operations in complex workflows, ensuring tasks are performed in the correct order.

---

3. Topological Sorting in DAGs

Topological sorting is a process used to order the nodes of a **DAG** in a way that respects the direction of edges. Specifically, for every directed edge **u** → **v**, **u** will appear before **v** in the sorted order.

There are two main algorithms for topological sorting:

- **Kahn's Algorithm** (based on in-degree)

- **Depth-First Search (DFS)**

Let's explore both approaches.

a. Kahn's Algorithm (Using In-Degree):

1. Calculate the **in-degree** (number of incoming edges) for each node.
2. Nodes with an in-degree of 0 are independent (i.e., they can be processed first).
3. Add all nodes with in-degree 0 to a queue and process them, reducing the in-degree of their neighbors.
4. Repeat the process until all nodes are processed.

Kahn's Algorithm in Python:

python

```python
from collections import deque

def topological_sort_kahn(graph):
    in_degree = {node: 0 for node in graph}  # Initialize in-degree for each node
    for node in graph:
        for neighbor in graph[node]:
            in_degree[neighbor] += 1  # Increase in-degree for each neighbor

    queue = deque([node for node in in_degree if in_degree[node] == 0])  # Nodes with no incoming edges
    sorted_order = []
```

```python
    while queue:
        node = queue.popleft()
        sorted_order.append(node)

        for neighbor in graph[node]:
            in_degree[neighbor] -= 1  # Decrease in-degree for each neighbor
            if in_degree[neighbor] == 0:
                queue.append(neighbor)  # Add to queue if no more incoming edges

    if len(sorted_order) == len(graph):
        return sorted_order
    else:
        raise ValueError("Graph has a cycle, topological sort not possible")

# Example graph (DAG)
graph = {
    'A': ['B', 'C'],
    'B': ['D'],
    'C': ['D'],
    'D': []
}

print(topological_sort_kahn(graph))
```

b. Topological Sorting Using Depth-First Search (DFS):

1. Perform a DFS traversal of the graph.
2. Mark each node as visited and push it to the stack once all its neighbors are processed.

3. The stack will contain the nodes in topologically sorted order when the DFS traversal is complete.

DFS-based Topological Sort in Python:

python

```python
def topological_sort_dfs(graph):
    visited = set()
    stack = []

    def dfs(node):
        if node in visited:
            return
        visited.add(node)
        for neighbor in graph[node]:
            dfs(neighbor)
        stack.append(node)

    for node in graph:
        if node not in visited:
            dfs(node)

    return stack[::-1]

# Example graph (DAG)
graph = {
    'A': ['B', 'C'],
    'B': ['D'],
    'C': ['D'],
```

```
 'D': []
}
```

```
print(topological_sort_dfs(graph))
```

---

4. Use Case: Job Scheduling Algorithms

One of the most common use cases for DAGs is in **job scheduling algorithms**, where the goal is to determine the order of tasks based on their dependencies. DAGs help ensure that tasks are executed in the correct order, with each task waiting for its dependent tasks to complete first.

Job Scheduling Example: Consider a set of tasks where some tasks depend on others. For example, task **A** must be completed before task **B**, and task **C** depends on both task **A** and task **B**. A DAG can represent these dependencies and help in scheduling the tasks in an order that respects the dependencies.

Real-World Job Scheduling Example:

- **CI/CD Pipelines**: In continuous integration and deployment, a DAG is used to define the sequence of jobs that need to run, such as unit tests, integration tests, and deployment. Some jobs depend on others, and a DAG ensures that jobs are executed in the right order.

- **Data Processing Pipelines**: Tools like Apache **Airflow** use DAGs to model workflows for data processing tasks, where one task may depend on the output of previous tasks, such as extracting, transforming, and loading data into a database.

In this chapter, we explored **Directed Acyclic Graphs (DAGs)** and their importance in modeling ordered tasks and dependencies. We covered how **topological sorting** can be applied to DAGs for efficient task scheduling, and we discussed real-world use cases like **job scheduling**, **dependency resolution**, and **workflow management**. With DAGs, systems can optimize execution orders and prevent circular dependencies that could cause deadlock or inefficient execution.

In the next chapter, we will explore **advanced graph algorithms**, diving deeper into concepts like **network flow algorithms**, **strongly connected components**, and other topics that build on the foundation of DAGs to solve even more complex real-world problems.

CHAPTER 16: INTRODUCTION TO HASHING

In this chapter, we will explore **hashing** and its critical role in improving the efficiency of data storage and retrieval. **Hashing** is a technique used to map data to a fixed-size value, often called a **hash code**, which makes it incredibly useful in the construction of **hash tables**. Hashing is widely used in many real-world applications, such as implementing dictionaries, caches, and databases, where fast data lookup is essential.

1. What is Hashing and Why Is It Important in Data Structures?

Hashing is a process of converting an input (often a string or object) into a fixed-size value, usually an integer, that represents the original input. This value is generated by a **hash function**, and the resulting hash is used to store and retrieve data efficiently.

- **Efficiency in Data Retrieval**: Hashing allows for **constant time complexity** ($O(1)$) for searching, inserting, and deleting elements, which is significantly faster than other data structures like arrays or linked lists, where these operations may take linear time (O(n)).

- **Real-World Applications**: Hashing is used in various applications that require quick data retrieval, including:
  - o **Dictionaries**: Storing key-value pairs where the key can be any object, and the value can be any data.
  - o **Caches**: Storing recently accessed data to speed up future access.
  - o **Databases**: Indexing data to quickly find records.

However, the core challenge with hashing is ensuring that the hash function distributes the data evenly to avoid collisions.

---

2. The Concept of Hash Functions

A **hash function** is an algorithm that takes an input (called the **key**) and maps it to an integer (the **hash value**), which can be used as an index in a hash table. A good hash function should have the following properties:

- **Deterministic**: The same input should always produce the same hash value.
- **Efficient**: It should be computationally fast to generate the hash.
- **Uniform Distribution**: It should distribute hash values evenly across the available space to minimize collisions.

- **Minimizing Collisions**: Ideally, the hash function should avoid generating the same hash value for different keys.

Here's a simple example of a hash function:

python

```
def simple_hash(key):
    return sum(ord(char) for char in key) % 100
```

In this case, the function calculates the sum of the ASCII values of each character in the key, and then takes the modulo with 100 to ensure the result fits into a hash table of size 100. Although this is a basic example, it demonstrates the concept of hashing.

---

3. Hash Collisions and How to Handle Them

A **collision** occurs when two different keys produce the same hash value. Collisions are inevitable due to the finite number of possible hash values. In these cases, the hash table must have a strategy to handle the collision and ensure that both keys can be stored and retrieved correctly.

There are two primary methods for handling collisions:

a. Open Addressing:

In open addressing, when a collision occurs, the algorithm tries to find another empty slot within the hash table to store the new key. The key is rehashed until an empty slot is found.

There are several strategies for open addressing:

- **Linear Probing**: When a collision occurs, the algorithm checks the next slot in the array. If that slot is occupied, it checks the next one, and so on until an empty slot is found.

  python

  ```python
  def linear_probe(table, key, value):
      index = simple_hash(key)
      while table[index] is not None:
          index = (index + 1) % len(table)
      table[index] = value
  ```

- **Quadratic Probing**: Instead of checking the next slot linearly, quadratic probing checks slots at increasing distances from the original hash, using a quadratic function to calculate the next index to try.
- **Double Hashing**: A second hash function is used to calculate an offset when a collision occurs, reducing clustering compared to linear or quadratic probing.

b. Chaining:

In chaining, each index in the hash table contains a **linked list** (or another container such as a set or another list) that holds all the values that hash to that index. When a collision occurs, the new key-value pair is simply added to the linked list at that index.

- **Advantages**: Chaining allows the hash table to handle a large number of collisions without needing to resize the table.
- **Disadvantages**: It can result in slower lookup times when many collisions occur at the same index, leading to a long linked list.

python

```python
class HashTable:
    def __init__(self, size):
        self.table = [[] for _ in range(size)]

    def hash_function(self, key):
        return simple_hash(key)

    def insert(self, key, value):
        index = self.hash_function(key)
        # Add key-value pair to the linked list at index
        self.table[index].append((key, value))

    def search(self, key):
        index = self.hash_function(key)
        for k, v in self.table[index]:
```

```
    if k == key:
        return v
    return None
```

In this implementation, each index in the table is a list that holds all key-value pairs whose keys hash to the same index.

---

4. Real-World Example: Storing Data in a Hash Table

Let's see how a **hash table** can be used in a practical application, such as implementing a **phone book** where names are the keys, and phone numbers are the values.

Here's a simple implementation of a phone book using a hash table with chaining to handle collisions:

python

```python
class PhoneBook:
    def __init__(self, size):
        self.table = [[] for _ in range(size)]

    def hash_function(self, name):
        return sum(ord(char) for char in name) % len(self.table)

    def add_contact(self, name, phone_number):
        index = self.hash_function(name)
        for i, (n, _) in enumerate(self.table[index]):
            if n == name:
```

```
        self.table[index][i] = (name, phone_number)   # Update existing
contact
            return
        self.table[index].append((name, phone_number)) # Add new contact

    def get_phone_number(self, name):
        index = self.hash_function(name)
        for n, phone in self.table[index]:
            if n == name:
                return phone
        return None


# Example usage
phone_book = PhoneBook(10)
phone_book.add_contact('Alice', '555-1234')
phone_book.add_contact('Bob', '555-5678')

print(phone_book.get_phone_number('Alice'))  # Output: 555-1234
print(phone_book.get_phone_number('Charlie')) # Output: None
```

In this example:

- The PhoneBook class uses a hash table with chaining to store contact names and their associated phone numbers.
- The hash_function converts the name into a hash code and maps it to an index in the table.
- The add_contact method handles collisions by appending to the list at the corresponding index, while the get_phone_number method looks up a name by checking the list at the corresponding index.

In this chapter, we introduced **hashing**, a powerful technique used in data structures for efficient data storage and retrieval. We discussed the concept of **hash functions**, the importance of uniform distribution, and the problem of **collisions**. We also explored two main collision resolution techniques: **open addressing** and **chaining**. Finally, we provided a real-world example of how hashing is used in a **phone book** application to demonstrate the efficiency and utility of hash tables in handling large datasets.

In the next chapter, we will explore **advanced hashing techniques**, including **dynamic resizing of hash tables**, and discuss their applications in building scalable systems like **caches** and **databases**.

CHAPTER 17: IMPLEMENTING HASH TABLES IN PYTHON

In this chapter, we will build a **hash table** from scratch in Python, exploring its core operations—**insert**, **search**, and **delete**—while also handling **hash collisions** effectively. We'll delve into the **time complexity** of hash table operations and understand how hash tables can be used in **practical applications**, such as **caching** and **database indexing**.

---

1. Building a Simple Hash Table from Scratch

A **hash table** is a data structure that stores key-value pairs and allows for fast retrieval based on the key. The core idea behind a hash table is to use a **hash function** to compute an index in an array, where the corresponding value will be stored. Python's built-in dict type is an implementation of a hash table, but in this chapter, we will manually implement a basic version of it to understand how it works under the hood.

To build a simple hash table:

1. Define the size of the hash table.
2. Create a list to store key-value pairs.
3. Implement a **hash function** to convert keys into valid indices in the table.

Let's implement a basic hash table:

python

```python
class HashTable:
    def __init__(self, size):
        self.size = size
        self.table = [None] * size  # Initialize the table with None values

    def hash_function(self, key):
        """A simple hash function that converts a string key into an index."""
        return sum(ord(char) for char in key) % self.size

    def insert(self, key, value):
        """Inserts a key-value pair into the hash table."""
        index = self.hash_function(key)
        if self.table[index] is None:
            self.table[index] = [(key, value)]  # Store a list of tuples
        else:
            # Handle collisions by appending to the list at the index
```

```python
        self.table[index].append((key, value))

    def search(self, key):
        """Search for a value by its key."""
        index = self.hash_function(key)
        if self.table[index] is not None:
            for item in self.table[index]:
                if item[0] == key:
                    return item[1]
        return None

    def delete(self, key):
        """Delete a key-value pair from the hash table."""
        index = self.hash_function(key)
        if self.table[index] is not None:
            for i, item in enumerate(self.table[index]):
                if item[0] == key:
                    del self.table[index][i]
                    return True
        return False
```

Here's a breakdown of how the hash table works:

- **insert**: The key is hashed using the hash_function. If no collision occurs at the computed index, the key-value pair is inserted. If a collision happens (i.e., the slot is already occupied), the key-value pair is appended to a list at that index.

- **search**: The function searches for the key by applying the hash function and then looks through the list at the corresponding index.

- **delete**: The function removes the key-value pair by first finding the corresponding index using the hash function and then deleting the pair from the list.

---

2. Hash Table Operations: Insert, Search, Delete

Let's explore the time complexity of the basic operations for this hash table implementation:

- **Insert**: In the average case, inserting a key-value pair is **O(1)** because the hash function directly computes an index. However, in the worst case (when all keys hash to the same index), the time complexity becomes **O(n)**, where n is the number of elements stored in the table.

- **Search**: Searching for a key is also **O(1)** on average. In the worst case, if all keys hash to the same index, the time complexity becomes **O(n)**.

- **Delete**: Deleting a key-value pair is **O(1)** on average, but it may degrade to **O(n)** if many keys hash to the same index and we need to search through a list to find the key.

---

3. Handling Hash Collisions in Python

As we've seen, **collisions** are an inherent issue in hash tables, and they occur when two different keys produce the same hash value. To handle collisions, we can use **chaining**, which stores multiple key-value pairs in a list at each index in the table, as demonstrated earlier.

However, in other implementations, we might use **open addressing**. In open addressing, when a collision occurs, the algorithm probes the table to find the next available slot.

Here's how open addressing can be implemented with **linear probing**:

python

```python
class HashTableOpenAddressing:
    def __init__(self, size):
        self.size = size
        self.table = [None] * size

    def hash_function(self, key):
        return sum(ord(char) for char in key) % self.size

    def insert(self, key, value):
        index = self.hash_function(key)
        # Linear probing to find the next available slot
        while self.table[index] is not None:
            index = (index + 1) % self.size
```

```
    self.table[index] = (key, value)


def search(self, key):
    index = self.hash_function(key)
    while self.table[index] is not None:
        if self.table[index][0] == key:
            return self.table[index][1]
        index = (index + 1) % self.size
    return None


def delete(self, key):
    index = self.hash_function(key)
    while self.table[index] is not None:
        if self.table[index][0] == key:
            self.table[index] = None
            return True
        index = (index + 1) % self.size
    return False
```

In **linear probing**, the function searches sequentially for the next available slot when a collision occurs. While this method works well in cases where collisions are rare, it can degrade the performance of the hash table when the load factor (the ratio of filled slots to total slots) is high.

4. Time Complexity of Hash Table Operations

Let's review the **time complexity** of hash table operations in various scenarios:

- **Insert**:
    - o Average Case: **O(1)**, assuming the hash function distributes keys evenly and there are few collisions.
    - o Worst Case: **O(n)** when all keys hash to the same index and the table uses a linked list or linear probing, which degenerates into a linear search.
- **Search**:
    - o Average Case: **O(1)**, with quick lookups using the hash index.
    - o Worst Case: **O(n)**, if a large number of keys hash to the same index.
- **Delete**:
    - o Average Case: **O(1)**, similar to search, the key can be found directly via hashing.
    - o Worst Case: **O(n)**, when collisions are handled with chains or linear probing, and the table is heavily populated.

To optimize performance, dynamic resizing (rehashing) is commonly used in practice. When the load factor exceeds a threshold (e.g., 70%), the hash table is resized, and all existing entries are rehashed and redistributed to new indices.

---

5. Practical Use Case: Caching, Database Indexing

Hash tables are incredibly useful in real-world scenarios where fast lookups are necessary. Below are some practical applications of hash tables:

Caching: Hash tables are widely used for caching, where frequently accessed data is stored temporarily to speed up retrieval. For example, web browsers use caching to store images, CSS files, and JavaScript code so that they don't need to be re-downloaded every time a user visits a webpage.

Here's a simple example of caching with a hash table:

python

```python
class Cache:
    def __init__(self, size):
        self.hash_table = HashTable(size)

    def get(self, key):
        return self.hash_table.search(key)

    def set(self, key, value):
        self.hash_table.insert(key, value)


cache = Cache(10)
cache.set('user1', {'name': 'Alice', 'age': 25})
print(cache.get('user1'))  # Output: {'name': 'Alice', 'age': 25}
```

Database Indexing: Hash tables are also used in databases for indexing. By creating an index based on certain key columns, the database can quickly look up records, improving search and retrieval times. For example, an index on a user_id column in a user database could enable fast lookups of user information based on the ID.

In this chapter, we built a basic hash table from scratch and explored its core operations—**insert**, **search**, and **delete**—while also addressing **collisions** using both **chaining** and **open addressing**. We also discussed the **time complexity** of hash table operations and explored real-world use cases such as **caching** and **database indexing**. Hash tables provide an efficient way to store and retrieve data and are used extensively in computer science for many practical applications.

In the next chapter, we will dive deeper into **advanced hash table techniques**, including **dynamic resizing**, and explore how hash tables can be optimized for even better performance.

CHAPTER 18: SORTING ALGORITHMS

Sorting is one of the most fundamental and widely used operations in computer science. Whether you're organizing a list of names in alphabetical order or sorting large datasets for efficient searching, understanding how sorting algorithms work is essential for any programmer.

In this chapter, we'll explore various **sorting algorithms**, focusing on the most commonly used ones: **Bubble Sort**, **Merge Sort**, and **Quick Sort**. We'll discuss the **time complexity** of these algorithms, how Python's built-in sorting functions work, and examine **real-world use cases** to understand when and why each sorting algorithm is used.

---

1. Overview of Sorting Algorithms

Sorting algorithms are used to arrange data in a specific order—typically **ascending** or **descending**. The most common types of sorting algorithms include:

- **Bubble Sort**: A simple but inefficient sorting algorithm. It repeatedly steps through the list, compares adjacent elements, and swaps them if they are in the wrong order.
- **Merge Sort**: A more efficient, **divide-and-conquer** algorithm. It splits the list into smaller sublists, recursively sorts each sublist, and then merges them back together in sorted order.
- **Quick Sort**: Another **divide-and-conquer** algorithm, but it selects a "pivot" element and partitions the list around the pivot, recursively sorting the sublists.

Let's take a closer look at each algorithm, starting with **Bubble Sort**.

---

2. Bubble Sort

Bubble Sort is one of the simplest sorting algorithms, but it's also one of the least efficient for large datasets. The basic idea is to repeatedly compare adjacent items in the list and swap them if they're in the wrong order.

Algorithm:

1. Traverse the list from the beginning to the end.

2. Compare each adjacent pair of elements.

3. If the current element is greater than the next element, swap them.

4. Repeat the process until no swaps are made during a full pass through the list.

Implementation:

python

```python
def bubble_sort(arr):
    n = len(arr)
    for i in range(n):
        swapped = False
        # Last i elements are already sorted
        for j in range(0, n-i-1):
            if arr[j] > arr[j+1]:
                arr[j], arr[j+1] = arr[j+1], arr[j]  # Swap if out of order
                swapped = True
        if not swapped:  # If no swaps were made, the list is sorted
            break
    return arr
```

Time Complexity:

- **Best Case** (when the list is already sorted): **O(n)**

- **Average and Worst Case: O(n^2)**, because every element needs to be compared with every other element in the list.

Real-World Use:

Bubble sort is not often used in practice due to its inefficiency. It's mainly taught for educational purposes to introduce the concept of sorting. However, it might be useful in very small datasets or when performance is not critical.

---

3. Merge Sort

Merge Sort is an efficient, stable, and widely used sorting algorithm that uses the **divide-and-conquer** strategy. It divides the list into smaller sublists, recursively sorts each sublist, and then merges the sublists into one sorted list.

Algorithm:

1. Divide the list into two halves.
2. Recursively sort each half.
3. Merge the sorted halves to produce a single sorted list.

Implementation:

python

```python
def merge_sort(arr):
    if len(arr) > 1:
        mid = len(arr) // 2  # Find the middle point
        left_half = arr[:mid]  # Divide the array into two halves
        right_half = arr[mid:]
```

```
merge_sort(left_half)  # Recursively sort the left half
merge_sort(right_half)  # Recursively sort the right half


i = j = k = 0


# Merge the two halves back into the original array
while i < len(left_half) and j < len(right_half):
    if left_half[i] < right_half[j]:
        arr[k] = left_half[i]
        i += 1
    else:
        arr[k] = right_half[j]
        j += 1
    k += 1


# Check if any element was left in either left_half or right_half
while i < len(left_half):
    arr[k] = left_half[i]
    i += 1
    k += 1


while j < len(right_half):
    arr[k] = right_half[j]
    j += 1
    k += 1


return arr
```

Time Complexity:

- **Best, Worst, and Average Case**: **O(n log n)**, because the list is divided in half at each level and merged at each level.

Real-World Use:

Merge sort is often used in applications where **stability** (preserving the relative order of equal elements) is important, such as in sorting large datasets that are stored in external memory (e.g., disk sorting).

---

4. Quick Sort

Quick Sort is another **divide-and-conquer** sorting algorithm that is often faster than merge sort on average. It works by selecting a **pivot element** and partitioning the list around it so that elements smaller than the pivot come before it and elements greater than the pivot come after it. The process is then repeated for the sublists.

Algorithm:

1. Choose a pivot element.
2. Partition the list so that elements smaller than the pivot are on the left and elements greater than the pivot are on the right.
3. Recursively apply the same process to the left and right sublists.

Implementation:

python

```
def quick_sort(arr):
    if len(arr) <= 1:
        return arr
    pivot = arr[len(arr) // 2]  # Choose the pivot (can be improved)
    left = [x for x in arr if x < pivot]  # Elements less than pivot
    middle = [x for x in arr if x == pivot]  # Elements equal to pivot
    right = [x for x in arr if x > pivot]  # Elements greater than pivot
    return quick_sort(left) + middle + quick_sort(right)
```

Time Complexity:

- **Best and Average Case**: **O(n log n)**, achieved when the pivot divides the list roughly in half.
- **Worst Case** (when the pivot is the smallest or largest element): **O(n^2)**, but this can be avoided with random pivot selection or other optimizations.

Real-World Use:

Quick sort is one of the most widely used algorithms in practice due to its **average-case efficiency** and **in-place sorting**. It's often used in scenarios where **time complexity** is a priority, such as sorting large datasets or arrays.

---

5. Python's Built-in Sorting Functions

Python provides **built-in sorting** functions that are optimized for performance. The sorted() function and the list.sort() method both use an algorithm called **Timsort**, which is a hybrid of **merge sort** and **insertion sort**.

- **sorted()**: Returns a new list with the sorted elements.
- **list.sort()**: Sorts the list in place and does not return a new list.

python

```
# Using sorted()
arr = [3, 1, 4, 1, 5, 9, 2, 6, 5]
sorted_arr = sorted(arr)
```

```
# Using list.sort()
arr.sort()
```

Both of these methods have a **time complexity of O(n log n)** and are very efficient for typical use cases.

---

6. When to Use Each Sorting Algorithm

Each sorting algorithm has its strengths and weaknesses. The choice of algorithm depends on factors like **input size**, **memory constraints**, and **specific requirements** (e.g., stability). Here's a quick guide:

- **Bubble Sort**: Use only for small datasets or educational purposes. Avoid for large datasets due to its O(n^2) time complexity.

- **Merge Sort**: Use when stability is required or when sorting large datasets, especially for external sorting (e.g., sorting files stored on disk).

- **Quick Sort**: Use for large datasets where time is a priority, and stability is not important. Quick sort is generally the fastest for in-memory sorting.

- **Python's built-in sorting**: Use this for most cases in Python, as it's highly optimized.

---

7. Real-World Example: Sorting Large Datasets Efficiently

In a real-world scenario, sorting large datasets efficiently is crucial. Suppose you have a large list of **user records** that need to be sorted based on the user's last name. You might consider using **merge sort** or **quick sort**, but if the data is stored on disk (external memory), **merge sort** would likely be the best choice.

For example, if you are building a **data analytics tool** that needs to sort logs from millions of users, using **Python's sorted() function** (which implements **Timsort**) would allow you to efficiently sort the data in memory without manually choosing an algorithm.

---

8. Conclusion

Sorting algorithms are at the heart of many programming tasks, and understanding their characteristics and trade-offs is crucial for selecting the right algorithm based on the problem at hand. In this chapter, we've covered the fundamentals of **Bubble Sort**, **Merge Sort**, and **Quick Sort**, examined their time complexities, and provided insights into when to use each one. Python's built-in sorting functions are often the most practical choice for most applications, but knowing how these algorithms work helps you make informed decisions when performance is a concern.

In the next chapter, we will explore **advanced algorithm techniques**, including **dynamic programming** and **greedy algorithms**, to solve more complex problems efficiently.

CHAPTER 19: SEARCHING ALGORITHMS

In this chapter, we will explore **searching algorithms**, which are essential for finding an element within a collection of data. Searching is one of the most fundamental operations in computer science, and there are various algorithms designed to solve this problem efficiently depending on the type of data structure and the scenario.

We will focus on two key searching algorithms: **Linear Search** and **Binary Search**, followed by a discussion of **Binary Search Trees (BST)** and **optimizations** for searching in sorted data.

---

1. Linear Search

Linear Search is the most straightforward searching algorithm. It works by sequentially checking each element in a collection until a match is found or the entire collection has been traversed.

Algorithm:

1. Start from the first element in the list.
2. Compare the current element with the target element.
3. If a match is found, return the index or position of the element.
4. If the element is not found after checking every item, return a failure indicator (e.g., None or -1).

Implementation:

python

```python
def linear_search(arr, target):
    for i, element in enumerate(arr):
        if element == target:
            return i  # Return the index of the element
    return -1  # Return -1 if element is not found
```

Time Complexity:

- **Best Case**: O(1) — when the target is found at the first position.
- **Worst Case**: O(n) — when the target is at the end or not in the list at all.

- **Average Case**: O(n), as it requires checking each element on average.

Linear search is useful when the dataset is small or unsorted. It's simple to implement and doesn't require any preprocessing. However, for larger datasets, other more efficient algorithms may be preferred.

---

2. Binary Search

Binary Search is a much more efficient searching algorithm compared to linear search, but it requires the dataset to be **sorted** beforehand. Binary search works by repeatedly dividing the search interval in half. If the target value is smaller than the middle element, the search continues in the lower half, and if it's larger, the search continues in the upper half.

Algorithm:

1. Begin with the middle element of the sorted list.
2. If the target value is equal to the middle element, return the index.
3. If the target value is less than the middle element, narrow the search to the left half.

4. If the target value is greater than the middle element, narrow the search to the right half.

5. Repeat the process until the target is found or the search interval is empty.

Implementation:

python

```python
def binary_search(arr, target):
    low, high = 0, len(arr) - 1
    while low <= high:
        mid = (low + high) // 2  # Find the middle index
        if arr[mid] == target:
            return mid  # Target found, return the index
        elif arr[mid] < target:
            low = mid + 1  # Target is in the right half
        else:
            high = mid - 1  # Target is in the left half
    return -1  # Return -1 if target is not found
```

Time Complexity:

- **Best Case**: $O(1)$ — when the target is found at the middle of the array.

- **Worst Case**: $O(\log n)$ — with each iteration, the search space is halved.

- **Average Case**: $O(\log n)$, as the search space is reduced by half with each comparison.

Real-World Use:

Binary search is a very efficient algorithm for searching in sorted arrays or lists. It is widely used in various applications, such as **finding elements in large datasets** (e.g., large databases), **looking up records**, and **searching in structured data** (e.g., names in a phonebook, items in a catalog).

---

3. Binary Search Trees (BST) and Search Optimizations

A **Binary Search Tree (BST)** is a data structure that maintains a sorted order of elements. Each node in a BST has a value, and the values in the left subtree are smaller, while the values in the right subtree are larger.

BSTs are used to implement efficient searching, insertion, and deletion operations, with **average time complexity of O(log n)** for these operations. However, the time complexity can degrade to O(n) if the tree becomes unbalanced (e.g., if elements are inserted in sorted order).

BST Search Algorithm:

The search operation in a BST follows a similar approach to binary search. Start from the root node and move left or right based on comparisons.

Implementation:

python

```python
class Node:
    def __init__(self, value):
        self.value = value
        self.left = None
        self.right = None


def insert(root, value):
    if root is None:
        return Node(value)
    if value < root.value:
        root.left = insert(root.left, value)
    else:
        root.right = insert(root.right, value)
    return root


def search_bst(root, target):
    if root is None or root.value == target:
        return root  # Found the target or reached a leaf
    if target < root.value:
        return search_bst(root.left, target)  # Search left subtree
    else:
        return search_bst(root.right, target)  # Search right subtree
```

Time Complexity:

- **Best Case**: O(log n) — when the tree is balanced and the target is found quickly.
- **Worst Case**: O(n) — if the tree degenerates into a linked list (e.g., elements are inserted in sorted order).

Real-World Use:

BSTs are ideal for applications where **frequent insertions, deletions, and lookups** are needed, such as maintaining **sorted records** in databases or implementing **search engines**. To optimize searching and ensure O(log n) time complexity, **self-balancing BSTs** like **AVL trees** or **Red-Black trees** are often used.

---

4. Implementing Searching Algorithms in Python

Now, let's look at how to implement the above searching algorithms in Python, along with some real-world use cases:

- **Linear Search**: This algorithm is best used when the dataset is small or unsorted. For example, searching for a **name** in a contact list.
- **Binary Search**: Binary search is ideal when the data is **sorted**. It can be used in scenarios like **looking up items** in a product catalog or **searching in sorted lists** of customer records.
- **Binary Search Tree (BST)**: Used when you need efficient insertion and deletion along with searching, such as in **databases** that need to frequently update records.

Example: Search in Large Databases:

In large-scale applications such as a **database system** or an **online search engine**, data is often indexed using a **binary search tree** or **hashing**. This allows for fast querying and retrieval of information. For example, in an e-commerce site, **product search** uses binary search trees to quickly find items based on a given attribute (e.g., product ID, price range).

---

5. Real-World Use Case: Searching in Large Databases

Imagine you are building a **movie database** where you need to search for movies based on **movie title**. In this case, you could use **binary search** to search for a movie in a sorted list or a **binary search tree (BST)** to manage and optimize the search queries.

Example:

python

```python
# List of movie titles, sorted alphabetically
movie_titles = ["Avatar", "The Dark Knight", "Inception", "Titanic", "The Matrix"]
movie_to_find = "Inception"

# Binary search to find the movie
index = binary_search(movie_titles, movie_to_find)

if index != -1:
    print(f"Movie found at index {index}")
else:
```

```
print("Movie not found")
```

For large datasets, this type of optimized search becomes crucial in providing fast and accurate search results.

Searching algorithms are fundamental to the efficiency of many applications. Whether you are looking for a **name in a list**, **product in a catalog**, or **record in a database**, choosing the right algorithm can significantly improve performance.

- **Linear search** is simple but inefficient for large datasets.
- **Binary search** offers fast searching in sorted datasets.
- **Binary Search Trees (BST)** and **self-balancing BSTs** provide efficient searching, insertion, and deletion for dynamic data.

In this chapter, we've explored how to implement searching algorithms in Python, and we discussed their applications in **real-world scenarios**, such as **searching in large databases**. In the next chapter, we will explore more advanced algorithm topics, including **dynamic programming** and **greedy algorithms**, which are often used to solve optimization problems efficiently.

CHAPTER 20: DYNAMIC PROGRAMMING

Dynamic Programming (DP) is a powerful algorithmic technique used for solving optimization problems by breaking them down into simpler subproblems. DP is often used in scenarios where a problem can be divided into overlapping subproblems, and solving each subproblem independently would result in redundant computations. This technique helps reduce the computational complexity by storing the results of subproblems to avoid re-calculation, leading to more efficient solutions.

In this chapter, we will introduce **dynamic programming**, explain its core concepts, and walk through common problems that can be solved using this technique. We will also look at two popular strategies in dynamic programming: **memoization** and **tabulation**.

Finally, we will explore real-world examples to understand how dynamic programming can optimize performance for large-scale problems.

---

1. Introduction to Dynamic Programming

Dynamic programming is a method used to solve problems by breaking them down into smaller, overlapping subproblems and storing the results of these subproblems to avoid redundant computations. It's particularly useful for problems that have **optimal substructure** (i.e., the optimal solution to the problem can be constructed efficiently from optimal solutions of its subproblems) and **overlapping subproblems** (i.e., the same subproblems are solved multiple times).

While recursion is often used for solving problems by repeatedly calling a function with smaller inputs, **dynamic programming** overcomes the inefficiencies of recursion by storing intermediate results in a **table** or **memoization**. This avoids redundant calls, which can make the solution more efficient.

Basic Steps in Dynamic Programming:

1. **Characterize the structure of an optimal solution**: Break down the problem into smaller subproblems.
2. **Define the value of the optimal solution**: Express the optimal solution in terms of subproblems.

3. **Recursively define the solution**: Use a recurrence relation to define the problem in terms of smaller subproblems.

4. **Compute the solution bottom-up**: Use memoization or tabulation to store results and solve the problem iteratively.

5. **Construct the final solution**: Combine the subproblem solutions to get the overall optimal solution.

---

2. Common Dynamic Programming Problems

Let's walk through two classic dynamic programming problems that illustrate the principles of DP: the **Fibonacci Series** and the **Knapsack Problem**.

Fibonacci Series

The Fibonacci sequence is a simple mathematical sequence where each number is the sum of the two preceding ones, starting from 0 and 1. The recursive approach to computing Fibonacci numbers results in a lot of redundant calculations, which makes it inefficient. Dynamic programming optimizes this by storing the results of previous calculations.

Recursive Solution (Inefficient):

python

```
def fibonacci(n):
```

```python
if n <= 1:
    return n
return fibonacci(n - 1) + fibonacci(n - 2)
```

Optimized Dynamic Programming Solution:

python

```python
# Memoization approach (top-down approach)
def fibonacci_memo(n, memo={}):
    if n <= 1:
        return n
    if n not in memo:
        memo[n] = fibonacci_memo(n - 1, memo) + fibonacci_memo(n - 2, memo)
    return memo[n]


# Tabulation approach (bottom-up approach)
def fibonacci_tab(n):
    dp = [0] * (n + 1)
    dp[1] = 1
    for i in range(2, n + 1):
        dp[i] = dp[i - 1] + dp[i - 2]
    return dp[n]
```

Time Complexity:

- **Recursive approach**: $O(2^n)$ — exponential time due to repeated calculations.
- **Memoization approach**: $O(n)$ — each Fibonacci number is calculated once.

- **Tabulation approach**: O(n) — fills an array iteratively with no recursion.

Knapsack Problem

The **Knapsack Problem** is a well-known optimization problem. Given a set of items, each with a weight and value, the goal is to determine the maximum value that can be obtained by selecting a subset of items such that their total weight does not exceed a given capacity.

The recursive approach for solving this problem involves trying every possible combination of items, leading to an exponential time complexity. Dynamic programming optimizes this by storing intermediate results.

Recursive Solution (Inefficient):

python

```python
def knapsack(weights, values, capacity, n):
    if n == 0 or capacity == 0:
        return 0
    if weights[n - 1] > capacity:
        return knapsack(weights, values, capacity, n - 1)
    return max(
        values[n - 1] + knapsack(weights, values, capacity - weights[n - 1], n - 1),
        knapsack(weights, values, capacity, n - 1)
    )
```

Optimized Dynamic Programming Solution:

python

```python
def knapsack_dp(weights, values, capacity):
    n = len(weights)
    dp = [[0] * (capacity + 1) for _ in range(n + 1)]

    for i in range(n + 1):
        for w in range(capacity + 1):
            if i == 0 or w == 0:
                dp[i][w] = 0
            elif weights[i - 1] <= w:
                dp[i][w] = max(values[i - 1] + dp[i - 1][w - weights[i - 1]], dp[i - 1][w])
            else:
                dp[i][w] = dp[i - 1][w]

    return dp[n][capacity]
```

Time Complexity:

- **Recursive approach**: $O(2^n)$ — exponential time due to repeated calculations.
- **Dynamic Programming approach**: $O(n * W)$ — where n is the number of items and W is the capacity of the knapsack.

---

3. Memoization vs Tabulation

Dynamic programming can be implemented using two main techniques: **memoization** and **tabulation**. Both techniques store intermediate results, but they differ in how they do so.

Memoization (Top-Down Approach):

- **Approach**: Start with the original problem and break it down recursively, storing results of subproblems in a cache (typically a dictionary or an array).
- **When to use**: When you prefer a top-down approach, i.e., solving the original problem first and recursively solving the subproblems.
- **Advantages**: Easier to implement and understand, especially for problems with natural recursive definitions.

Tabulation (Bottom-Up Approach):

- **Approach**: Start by solving the smallest subproblems and build up to the original problem iteratively, storing the results in a table (typically a 2D array).
- **When to use**: When you want to avoid recursion and prefer an iterative approach to solve the problem.
- **Advantages**: Avoids the overhead of recursion and is often more space-efficient because it avoids the stack depth associated with recursion.

Comparison:

Aspect	Memoization	Tabulation
Approach	Top-down (recursion)	Bottom-up (iteration)
Space Complexity	Can be higher due to recursion stack	Often lower, as no recursion stack is needed
Time Complexity	Same as tabulation for most problems	Same as memoization for most problems
Ease of Implementation	Easier to implement for recursive problems	Slightly more complex to implement for recursive problems

4. Real-World Examples

Dynamic programming is widely used in solving problems in areas such as **finance**, **bioinformatics**, **operations research**, and **network optimization**. Let's look at a few real-world examples where dynamic programming is applied:

- **Optimizing Investment Portfolio (Knapsack)**: You can use dynamic programming to solve the **knapsack problem** in portfolio management, where the goal is to maximize the return on investment subject to constraints like budget, risk, and asset allocation.

- **String Matching (Longest Common Subsequence)**: Dynamic programming is used in bioinformatics to find similarities between DNA or protein sequences using algorithms like the **Longest Common Subsequence** (LCS). This helps identify patterns and relationships in biological data.
- **Shortest Path in Networks (Dijkstra's Algorithm)**: Dynamic programming is often used in network routing algorithms, where the goal is to find the shortest path between nodes in a graph. This is essential in applications like **GPS navigation** and **internet routing**.

Dynamic programming is a key technique for solving problems with optimal substructure and overlapping subproblems. By using memoization or tabulation, we can significantly improve the efficiency of algorithms that would otherwise have exponential time complexity.

- **Memoization** is great for problems with a natural recursive structure.
- **Tabulation** is ideal when you want to solve problems iteratively and avoid recursion.

In this chapter, we've covered dynamic programming fundamentals, including common problems like the **Fibonacci sequence** and

Knapsack problem, and explored the differences between **memoization** and **tabulation**. We also saw real-world examples of how dynamic programming can optimize large-scale problems, from **investment portfolios** to **genetic sequence matching**. Understanding dynamic programming is essential for solving many complex problems efficiently, and it's a technique that every programmer should have in their toolkit.

CHAPTER 21: BEST PRACTICES FOR IMPLEMENTING DATA STRUCTURES

When it comes to implementing data structures in Python, ensuring both **efficiency** and **readability** is crucial for producing high-quality, maintainable code. The right data structure can dramatically improve the performance of your algorithms, while the wrong one can lead to inefficiencies, increased complexity, and difficult-to-maintain code. In this chapter, we'll explore **best practices** for implementing data structures effectively, how to avoid common pitfalls, and how to balance efficiency with code readability.

We'll also delve into the important aspects of **memory management**, **performance considerations**, and **choosing the right data structure** for a given problem, along with how to make your Python code both **clean** and **maintainable**.

---

1. Common Pitfalls and How to Avoid Them

Implementing data structures can be challenging, especially when it comes to handling edge cases, ensuring efficiency, and keeping the code clear. Below are some common pitfalls developers face when working with data structures and how to avoid them:

Pitfall 1: Inefficient Data Structure Choices

Choosing the wrong data structure can lead to poor performance. For instance, using a **list** for frequent **insertions** and **deletions** can cause O(n) time complexity, while a **deque** or **linked list** would provide O(1) time for these operations. It's important to understand the trade-offs involved in choosing a particular data structure.

Best Practice:

- Always consider the operations you will be performing most frequently (insertion, deletion, access, etc.) and choose the data structure accordingly.
- Use lists when you need fast random access, and deques or linked lists when you need fast insertions and deletions.

Pitfall 2: Not Handling Edge Cases

Data structures often require careful handling of edge cases like empty structures, bounds checking, and corner cases during traversal.

Best Practice:

- Always consider edge cases, such as **empty lists**, **null values**, or **out-of-bounds accesses**. Implement safety checks to avoid errors that can cause unexpected behavior or crashes.

Pitfall 3: Ignoring Memory Management

Some data structures, particularly those that involve references or pointers (like linked lists or trees), can be memory-intensive if not managed properly.

Best Practice:

- Be mindful of **memory leaks** in custom implementations, especially when using **linked structures**. Python's **garbage collection** typically handles memory, but be cautious with circular references or manually managed memory.

Pitfall 4: Overcomplicating Data Structures

While it might be tempting to create overly complex data structures, this can complicate the design and increase debugging efforts.

Best Practice:

- Aim for **simplicity** in design. Start with basic, well-known data structures like arrays or dictionaries, and build up to more complex structures only when needed.

2. Efficient Memory Management with Data Structures

Memory efficiency is a key consideration when implementing data structures. While Python automatically handles memory management via **garbage collection**, it is still important to understand how different data structures can affect memory usage.

Understanding Memory Usage in Python:

- **Lists** and **tuples** are quite memory-efficient for small-scale data, but may become inefficient when holding large amounts of data or when performing frequent insertions and deletions.
- **Dictionaries** use a **hash table** internally, and while they are fast for lookups, they also consume more memory due to the storage of key-value pairs.
- **Sets** have a similar structure to dictionaries but only store unique elements, which can sometimes make them more memory efficient than lists when working with unique data.

Best Practices:

- **Choose the right data structure for your data size**. For small to medium-sized datasets, Python's built-in data structures (lists, sets, dictionaries) are often fine, but as data scales, you may need to use more memory-efficient structures like **arrays** (using the array module) or specialized libraries like **NumPy** for large numerical datasets.

- **Avoid using excessive copies of large structures**. For example, use a **generator** instead of a list when processing large amounts of data to avoid loading everything into memory at once.
- **Garbage collection** in Python handles memory management automatically, but you should still be mindful of **circular references** in your own code when implementing custom data structures.

---

3. *Choosing the Right Data Structure for the Task at Hand*

One of the most important skills in data structure design is selecting the right data structure based on the specific requirements of the task. Let's consider different scenarios and how to approach choosing the best data structure.

Scenario 1: Frequent Access and Random Indexing

- **Best Choice**: **List** or **Tuple**
- **Reason**: Lists offer O(1) access to elements by index. Tuples provide similar benefits with the added advantage of being immutable.

Scenario 2: Frequent Insertions and Deletions

- **Best Choice**: **Deque** (double-ended queue) or **Linked List**
- **Reason**: Lists and arrays are inefficient for insertions and deletions, as they require shifting elements. **Deques** (available via Python's collections.deque) and **Linked Lists** provide O(1) time complexity for insertions and deletions from the ends.

Scenario 3: Fast Lookups or Key-Value Pair Storage

- **Best Choice**: **Dictionary**
- **Reason**: Python's dictionaries are implemented as hash tables and provide O(1) average time complexity for lookups, insertions, and deletions. They are ideal when you need efficient key-value pair access.

Scenario 4: Maintaining Order and Uniqueness

- **Best Choice**: **Set**
- **Reason**: Sets automatically handle uniqueness and provide O(1) average time complexity for insertions and lookups. If order doesn't matter, sets are a great choice.

Scenario 5: Graph Representation

- **Best Choice**: **Adjacency List** (using dictionaries or lists) or **Adjacency Matrix**
- **Reason**: Graphs are commonly represented as adjacency lists for sparse graphs and adjacency matrices for dense graphs. The adjacency list is often more memory-efficient when storing graphs with many nodes but few edges.

Scenario 6: Priority-Based Task Scheduling

- **Best Choice**: **Heap** (Min-Heap or Max-Heap)
- **Reason**: Heaps are great for maintaining a priority queue where the highest or lowest priority element is always at the top. Python provides a heapq library for efficient heap operations.

---

4. Performance Considerations and Trade-offs

When selecting a data structure, performance is a key consideration. There are always trade-offs between time complexity, space complexity, and ease of use. Let's look at a few important considerations:

- **Space vs. Time Complexity**: Many algorithms and data structures trade space for time or vice versa. For example, a **hash table** (dictionary) provides fast access but uses more memory, while an **array** or **list** uses less memory but can be slower for certain operations (like searching).

- **Amortized Time Complexity**: Some operations, like list append or dictionary insertions, may seem slow in the worst case but have better average performance when amortized across multiple operations. Always analyze the average-case complexity when choosing a data structure.

- **Access Patterns**: Consider how you will interact with the data. If you need random access to elements, **arrays** or **hash tables** are best. If you need to process items in order or with a specific traversal, **queues**, **stacks**, or **trees** might be better choices.

---

5. Code Readability and Maintainability in Python

While efficiency is critical, code readability and maintainability are just as important, especially in collaborative environments. Writing clear, understandable code makes it easier for others (and your future self) to modify and debug the implementation.

Best Practices:

- **Use Descriptive Variable Names**: Choose meaningful names for variables, classes, and functions. Avoid single-letter names like x or y unless they are loop counters.

- **Document Your Code**: Always add comments or docstrings to explain complex logic or the purpose of functions and classes. Python's **PEP 257** provides guidelines for writing docstrings.

- **Modular Design**: Keep functions and classes small and focused on one task. This makes it easier to test and modify them independently.

- **Follow PEP 8**: Adhere to Python's **PEP 8** style guide for consistency in formatting, naming conventions, and code organization.

- **Avoid Premature Optimization**: Don't optimize too early—first, make sure the code works and is clear. Only optimize when you have identified real performance bottlenecks.

Choosing and implementing the right data structure is a critical part of writing efficient and maintainable code. By following the best practices outlined in this chapter—avoiding common pitfalls, managing memory effectively, choosing the right structure for the task at hand, and optimizing for performance—you can ensure that your code is both efficient and easy to understand.

Remember that **simplicity** and **clarity** often lead to better long-term solutions, and performance should only be optimized when necessary. By adhering to these principles, you'll be able to implement robust and performant data structures in Python, ultimately leading to better software design and development.

CHAPTER 22: REAL-WORLD APPLICATIONS OF DATA STRUCTURES

In this final chapter, we'll explore how data structures are applied in real-world systems. The design of complex software systems heavily depends on choosing the right data structures to meet performance and efficiency needs. Data structures are not just theoretical concepts—they are foundational elements that power many real-world applications such as databases, search engines, social networks, file systems, and more.

This chapter will provide several **case studies** that demonstrate how different data structures are utilized in these systems. We will also discuss how multiple data structures can be integrated into larger, more complex systems to achieve high efficiency, scalability, and robustness. Finally, we'll end with **final thoughts** on mastering data structures and algorithms and how you can continue to build on the knowledge you've gained in this book.

---

1. How Data Structures Are Used in Real-World Applications

Data structures are at the heart of many modern applications, enabling them to store, retrieve, manipulate, and organize data efficiently. Let's take a look at how specific data structures are used in real-world systems:

Arrays and Lists

Arrays and lists are fundamental data structures used to store and manipulate sequences of data. They are used in:

- **Databases**: In-memory databases or data storage systems often use arrays to store rows or records.
- **Web Development**: Lists are commonly used for storing user-generated content, such as blog posts, tweets, or forum threads.

Stacks and Queues

Stacks and queues are widely used in scenarios where tasks are processed in a specific order.

- **Stacks**: Used in undo/redo functionality in text editors or web browsers. They are also essential for **parsing expressions** and evaluating mathematical formulas in compilers and interpreters.
- **Queues**: Used in task scheduling, job queues, print spooling, and in **breadth-first search** (BFS) algorithms in graph traversal.

Linked Lists

Linked lists, both singly and doubly, provide efficient insertions and deletions compared to arrays and lists.

- **Memory Management**: Many memory allocation schemes (such as garbage collection) use linked lists to manage memory blocks.
- **Music or Video Players**: Implementing playlists as a linked list allows for easy traversal, insertion, and deletion of items.

Trees and Binary Search Trees (BST)

Trees, particularly binary search trees, are used extensively in scenarios that require hierarchical data representation.

- **Databases**: **B-trees** and **B+ trees** are used for indexing in databases, allowing fast search, insert, and delete operations.

- **Search Engines**: Search engines use inverted indexes that resemble tree structures to quickly locate documents containing query terms.
- **File Systems**: Many modern file systems (e.g., NTFS, HFS+) use trees to represent the directory structure and manage files efficiently.

Heaps and Priority Queues

Heaps are particularly useful for managing dynamic data that needs to be processed in order of priority.

- **Task Scheduling**: Operating systems use heaps in priority queues to manage the scheduling of tasks based on priority levels.
- **Pathfinding Algorithms**: Dijkstra's and A* algorithms use heaps to efficiently find the shortest path in graphs.

Hash Tables

Hash tables are incredibly efficient for situations requiring fast lookups, insertions, and deletions.

- **Databases**: Used for indexing in key-value stores (e.g., Redis) and NoSQL databases (e.g., MongoDB).
- **Caching**: Hash tables are the foundation of caching mechanisms, where fast retrieval of frequently used data is required.

Graphs

Graphs model relationships between entities in networks, making them fundamental for applications that involve complex relationships.

- **Social Networks**: Graphs are used to represent users as nodes and connections as edges, enabling features like friend recommendations and social graph traversal.
- **Routing and Navigation**: Algorithms like **Dijkstra's** and *A search** algorithms are used in GPS and navigation systems to find the shortest path between two points.

---

2. Case Studies

Here, we will walk through a few detailed case studies of real-world applications, demonstrating how various data structures are employed in their design.

Case Study 1: Databases

Databases, whether relational or NoSQL, rely heavily on a combination of data structures to efficiently store and query data.

- **B-trees and B+ Trees**: In a relational database like **MySQL** or **PostgreSQL**, B-trees are used for indexing, enabling fast lookup of records.

- **Hash Tables**: NoSQL databases like **MongoDB** use hash tables to store and retrieve data by key.
- **Linked Lists**: In some cases, linked lists are used in **transaction logs** to track changes to data records for **ACID compliance**.

Case Study 2: Search Engines

Search engines like **Google** use a variety of data structures to crawl the web, index content, and return relevant search results.

- **Graphs**: The web itself is represented as a graph, where each webpage is a node and hyperlinks are edges.
- **Inverted Indexes**: An inverted index is a hash table that maps a word (or key term) to a list of documents that contain it.
- **Priority Queues**: Used in algorithms like **PageRank** to prioritize pages based on factors like relevance and importance.

Case Study 3: Social Networks

Social networks like **Facebook, Twitter,** and **LinkedIn** use complex graph-based models to represent users, posts, likes, and relationships.

- **Graphs**: Users are represented as nodes, and their relationships (friendships, followers) are edges.

- **Hash Tables**: Used to quickly look up user profiles, posts, and metadata.

- **Queues**: Used in the **newsfeed algorithms** to manage and display posts in the correct order.

Case Study 4: File Systems

Modern file systems like **NTFS** (Windows) and **HFS+** (MacOS) use trees to manage file storage.

- **Trees**: Files are organized in a hierarchical structure (directories and subdirectories), which is often represented as a tree. **B-trees** are used for managing directory structures and file metadata.

- **Linked Lists**: Linked lists are used in certain file system implementations for managing free space (e.g., free blocks on disk).

---

3. Integrating Different Data Structures into Complex Systems

In practice, many applications combine different data structures to achieve the best results. Here are a few examples of how multiple data structures can work together in a single system:

Case Example: Task Scheduling System

A task scheduling system that prioritizes tasks based on their deadlines or importance might use:

- A **heap** (priority queue) to manage tasks based on priority.
- A **hash table** to store tasks by unique task IDs for fast retrieval.
- A **queue** to handle tasks waiting for execution in the correct order.

Case Example: Web Crawler

A web crawler that indexes web pages might use:

- A **graph** to represent the relationship between web pages.
- A **queue** to manage URLs to be visited.
- A **hash table** to keep track of visited URLs and prevent redundant crawling.

By integrating data structures such as queues, heaps, and graphs, a system can achieve higher performance, scalability, and reliability.

---

4. Final Thoughts and Next Steps for Mastering Data Structures and Algorithms

Congratulations! You've now gained a strong foundation in the implementation and application of data structures and algorithms in Python. Mastering these concepts will greatly enhance your ability to design efficient software systems, solve complex problems, and optimize for performance.

Here are some next steps to continue building on your knowledge:

- **Practice**: Continue to solve problems on platforms like **LeetCode, HackerRank**, and **Codeforces** to improve your problem-solving skills and reinforce your understanding of data structures and algorithms.
- **Projects**: Start building larger-scale projects that involve complex data manipulations, such as creating a **web scraper**, a **task manager**, or a **social network**.
- **Advanced Topics**: After mastering the fundamentals, dive into more advanced topics such as **graph algorithms**, **dynamic programming**, and **parallel computing**.
- **Contribute to Open Source**: Working on open-source projects that involve large data structures can be a great way to gain hands-on experience and learn from experienced developers.

With practice and dedication, you can continue to deepen your understanding of data structures and algorithms, and become proficient in creating high-performance software that solves real-world challenges.

Conclusion

In this chapter, we've seen how data structures power real-world systems and how you can apply them effectively in different scenarios. By mastering data structures and algorithms, you'll be equipped to design efficient, scalable, and high-performing applications that meet the needs of today's complex software environments.

Now, armed with knowledge of Python's data structures, the theory behind them, and how they are used in practical applications, you're ready to tackle a wide range of real-world problems and continue growing as a developer. Happy coding!

www.ingramcontent.com/pod-product-compliance
Lightning Source LLC
Chambersburg PA
CBHW070944050326
40689CB00014B/3334